VEGETARIAN DINING IN NYC
(and not just the places the yuppies like)

4TH EDITION
By Arthur S. Brown & Barbara Holmes

© 1994 By Arthur S. Brown & Barbara Holmes

Callaloo Press

ISBN: 0-9635338-2-7

Library of Congress
Catalogue Card Number: 92-075504

Published by
Callaloo Press
P.O. Box 845
Brooklyn, N.Y. 11230
(718) 434–3180
E–Mail VEGMAVEN@AOL.COM

ACKNOWLEDGMENTS

Our thanks to:

- Wil Tucker: your research on Wheelchair Access and Hours was inestimable.

- Teresa Agrillo: a multi-talented woman who provided high-quality proofreading.

- Russ Walter, author of "The Secret Guide to Computers" (the best all 'round computer book ever written). His help was invaluable at the times when our word processor behaved more like a food processor – slicing and dicing our data.

- Everyone who wrote or called with a new restaurant they discovered that "really should be in our book," or to tell us that a particular restaurant's quality had changed. Your input was extremely valuable.

- And last, but most certainly not least, the thousands of wonderful people who bought the 3rd, 2nd, or 1st editions. Your encouragement and support has kept us going.

DEDICATION

We dedicate this work to vegetarians everywhere, anyone who is trying to eat less meat for whatever reason, and to our daughter Jasmine, who would still never eat a cat.

Arthur S. Brown & Barbara Holmes

December, 1994

TABLE OF CONTENTS

INTRODUCTION

Well, Hi-de-ho, neighbor and welcome to the *4th Edition of Vegetarian Dining in NYC (and not just the places the yuppies like)*.

Since the 3rd Edition, we've bid farewell to many old favorites that have closed, and offered big N.Y. greets to many new faces. We've joined the race to pre–literacy by adding symbols after each review, so you'll be able to discern at a glance a particular restaurant's commitment to many important items.

The focus of this book is choice. The gang wants to eat at the local diner, which means that you, as a vegetarian, get a dry English Muffin or some Cole Slaw; or you're in an unfamiliar neighborhood and you don't know what's around.

The criterion for inclusion in our guide is that a restaurant either be completely vegetarian or that it offer a good number of vegetarian entrees. Beyond that, the restaurants chosen represent the subjective tastes of the authors.

For clarification's sake, when we say "vegetarian," we generally mean lacto–ovo–vegetarian. We chose this broad definition in a deliberate effort to reach out to the greatest number of people. We wanted to make it as easy as possible for everyone to try quality, meatless dining. However, every restaurant in our guide has at least something for vegans. Consequently, we believe that we've assembled the most complete guide to where a vegetarian or vegan in New York City can eat.

As the subtitle "not just the places the yuppies like" implies, we tried to single out, in particular, those restaurants that are less expensive and/or in the New York neighborhoods that other guidebooks ignore.

Since our book contains no advertising, we did not feel obliged to give anyone a favorable review when we didn't feel it was warranted or to withhold one when we felt it was deserved. We called it as we saw it, and the opinions are our own.

Meatless food is on the march! Since the 3rd Edition, vegetarian and vegetarian–friendly restaurants have been opening in our city at an exhilarating rate. As a sweetly ironic coda to the recent conflicts in Crown Heights, Brooklyn, the two groups that have opened the greatest number of vegetarian restaurants this past year are Kosher/Dairy and West Indian/Rasta. Why *can't* we all just get along?

We found, in the course of our research, that there are quite a few places in this city calling themselves vegetarian that under even moderate scrutiny should not be so called—and of course all sorts of nonsense is still being sold under the banner of "health food." Nevertheless, if you're hankering for a good vegetarian or vegan meal, you *can* get it in New York—and you now know exactly where to go.

As always, we've tried to make this guide as thorough as possible, but if we've left out your favorite restaurant, or if you have something to say, please drop us a line. We love to hear from you. That's how we improve–feedback! Our mailing address is: *P.O. Box 845, Midwood Station, Brooklyn, N.Y. 11230.* Our E–Mail address is: *Vegmaven@aol.com* for all you computer–literate types.

A word about the new information regarding accessibility to people in wheelchairs. We tried to provide the most accurate information possible regarding a variety of situations, the optimal situation, of course, being a ramp at the entrance and a large, accessible bathroom. Most of the restaurants we gave the Wh symbol to had this. Some of the "wheelchair accessible" restaurants had a few steps at the entrance and no ramp. All of these stated that employees would be happy to help carry a disabled person down the stairs. And then, there were some that had wheelchair access but no viable bathroom. If there was any doubt whatsoever, we left off the symbol altogether. Bottom line: use our info as a guideline and CALL FIRST. If it's in your nature, and a restaurant is not accessible, check out the Americans with Disabilities Act of 1989 and proceed accordingly.

Our heartfelt thanks to the thousands of wonderful people who bought previous editions. Your encouragement has kept us going.

Remember, restaurants open and close all the time, so it's always wise to call first.

We hope you find our guide both helpful and enjoyable, and we look forward to your feedback. Real food for real people.

Happy eating!

KEY TO PRICES

We've broken down price into four categories—Inexpensive, Moderate, Moderate–Expensive, and Expensive. Since a primary focus of our book is the promotion of *low–cost* dining, our parameters are lower than those of certain "Brand–X" guidebooks that shall remain nameless. Besides which, they don't even get out the dirt.

In any event, here are our definitions:

For the average price of an entree without any extras (dessert, booze, coffee, fingerbowl, or hula dancers):

Inexpensive: $6.00 and below

Moderate: $6.00–$9.00

Moderate–Expensive: $9.00–$12.00

Expensive: $12.00 and above

WHY EAT LESS MEAT?

YOUR HEALTH

In a paper published by The American Dietetic Association citing its position on vegetarian diets, it was stated that "It may be easier, as well as more acceptable, for some individuals to meet the Dietary Guidelines for Americans by following a vegetarian diet rather than a non vegetarian diet."[1] The newly revised Dietary Guidelines published November 5, 1990, by the United States Department of Agriculture have increased recommendations for individuals regarding consumption of vegetables to three to five servings per day, and of fruits to two to four servings per day.[3] Americans are also advised to consume more fiber and less animal fats. Following these dietary guidelines will reduce the risk of several degenerative diseases, including coronary artery disease and cancer, the top two disease–related causes of death in this country. A significant number of scientific studies have correlated the risk reduction of numerous degenerative diseases with vegetarian diets.[1]

WORLD HUNGER

As Frances Moore Lappé pointed out in <u>Diet for a Small Planet</u>, 16 pounds of grain and/or soybeans are required to produce 1 pound of beef in the United States. More grain is fed to livestock than to people, and the meat produced in third–world countries is normally exported or eaten by the rich minority. The gap between the rich and the poor is widening.[4]

THE ENVIRONMENT

Production of beef also profoundly affects our environment. For every pound of beef they yield, cattle emit a third of a pound of methane. According to Alan Durning, senior researcher at the Worldwatch Institute (an environmental research group), this is one of the major causes of the greenhouse effect, which is warming the earth and adversely affecting our climate.

Destruction of rain forests to provide grazing land reduces the earth's ability to produce oxygen. Livestock production also destroys arable land. Twenty–seven million acres of public American land have already been converted to desert as a result of commercial livestock production.[5]

Meat as the central component of human diet is a relatively recent phenomenon. Humans have survived throughout the millennia primarily on plant–centered diets. This type of eating truly does seem to be more natural because historically, animal foods were not as reliably obtainable as plant foods. The authors of this book advocate a return to a more traditional plant–centered diet.[4]

SOME SUGGESTIONS

Any diet, whether vegetarian or not, can be either healthful or not, depending on a number of factors. Just as eating too many animal foods can contribute to health risks, a very limited or poorly planned vegetarian or vegan diet can also be detrimental.[1]

When considering pitfalls to a vegetarian or vegan diet, the first nutrient that comes to mind is vitamin B–12. B–12 is not present in any food of plant origin. Although B–12 is cultivated in certain fermented foods such as tempeh, what is actually grown are primarily certain B–12 analogs that do not function as vitamins. A nutritional yeast grown on a B–12–rich medium is a better source of the nutrient. While vitamin B–12 deficiency is rare, it is a possibility for a longtime, non–supplemented vegan.[1]

Another area of specific concern is proper nutrition for the vegetarian child, particularly in late infancy and toddlerhood. Between the ages of 6–18 months, deficiencies can occur among children following vegan or vegan–like diets. Nutrients to be concerned with are calories, protein, vitamin D and B–12, calcium, phosphorus, zinc, and iron. Because a child's stomach capacity is limited, a high fiber diet is not necessarily warranted when not accompanied by sufficient calories.[2]

Iron is particularly crucial to the developing child because of its relationship to brain development and function. Substances called phytates and oxylates that inhibit the availability of iron from plant sources are often abundant in a whole foods diet. Fortunately, vitamin C enhances the absorption of iron from plant sources. In one study, vitamin C intake by vegetarians was found to be almost twice that of non–vegetarians. Another way to increase iron intake is by the use of cast iron cookware.[2]

Try to learn all that you can about nutrition, so that you and your family can make the right choices.

REFERENCES

1   "Position of the American Dietetic Association:
    Vegetarian Diets–technical support paper." *Journal of the
    American Dietetic Association*, Vol. 88. No. 3, March
    1988.

2   Dwyer, J.T., Jacobs, C., "Vegetarian children: appropriate
    and inappropriate diets," *American Journal of Clinical
    Nutrition*, Vol. 48: pp. 811–8, 1988.

3   Webb, D., "Eating Well," *New York Times*, 7 Nov. 1990,
    pg. C3.

4   Lappé, F.M., *Diet for a Small Planet*, New York:
    Ballantine Books, 1982, pp. 9, 12–13, 68.

5   Bloyd–Peshkin, S., "Mumbling About Meat," *Vegetarian
    Times*, Oct. 1991, pp. 66–68.

KEY TO SYMBOLS*

Booze

Child–Friendly

Credit Cards

Kosher

Macrobiotic

Music or Entertainment

Organically raised products used here O

Places my cousin Melvin likes **Me**

Smoking Permitted

Veggie–Friendly **VF**

Vegetarian **V**

Vegan **Ve**

Wheelchair Accessible

*For a deeper discussion of this section, please consult "Man & His Symbols" by C.G. Jung.

ABYSSINIA

35 Grand Street
(Between 6th Avenue & West Broadway)
(212) 226–5959

If you've never eaten authentic Ethiopian food, you should. You sit around a large wicker table inside of which is placed a large tray of Injera (a crepe–like flatbread). Your food is served to you on top of this "bread." To eat, you tear off pieces of the Injera and sop up your food with it. Some vegetarian items include Azefa Wot (a Lentil dish with Onions and Ginger), Shuro (a delicious puree of Chickpeas, Garlic, and Tomatoes) and Yegomen Wot (Kale and Potatoes sautéed with Onions, Green Peppers and Spices). If you have a kid who still eats with their hands, bring them cuz that's how Ethiopian food is eaten. Sooner or later, somebody drinks too much honey wine and falls off their three–legged chair. Great fun, educational, deeelicious, and a good number of vegetarian dishes.

Monday–Friday: 6:00pm–11:00pm
Saturday and Sunday: 1:00pm–11:30pm

Moderate

VF

AMERICAN CAFÉ

160 Broadway
(Near Maiden Lane)
(212) 732–1426

Great little kosher dairy joint in the heart of the financial district. For those who don't know, to be certified kosher (which is a very strictly observed process) an establishment or kitchen must exclude any and all animal products (except milk, eggs, and certain types of fish). Great news if you're a lacto–ovo vegetarian, good news if you're a vegan. Veggie burgers made with vegetables and beans, and served on a 7–grain English muffin, Vegetable Chili over Brown Rice, and much more (including some great Israeli staples like Hummus, Babaganoush and Falafel). "Rick, you've got to save me!" You've got to hide the letters of transit!" "Sorry pal, the problems of three little people don't amount to a hill of beans in this world."

Monday–Thursday: 7:00am–8:00pm
Friday: 7:00am–3:00pm
Saturday and Sunday: Closed

Inexpensive

V ✡

ANGELICA KITCHEN

300 East 12th Street
(Between 1st & 2nd Avenues)
(212) 228–2909

Strictly Vegan, mostly Macrobiotic, quite ascetic restaurant with a vast, varied, and delicious menu. Formerly on Saint Marks place near Second Avenue, the space on 12th Street is light and airy like a macrobiotic eclair. OK, here's what you do—

have a seat at the communal table next to all the other serious people—careful–don't smile or express anything resembling happiness. Next, order some really good food. If you feel like an appetizer (funny, you don't look like an appetizer) you might try the following. The freshly baked corn bread with Tahini Spread or Carrot Butter is delicious, as is the Homemade Sauerkraut, and the Vegetable Paté. For your entree, try a Dragon Bowl (assorted vegetables, Beans, Rice, Seaweed, Salad, etc. in a beautiful bowl with a dragon at the bottom). The Soba with Tahini Sauce is great too (just a touch of horseradish)–and lots more! After your meal, try a calming glass of Mu Tea–a macrobiotic staple. All told, in spite of the serious atmosphere, Angelica's is the model for delicious, healthy food.

Seven days: 11:30am–10:30pm

Moderate

Ve　　🌓　　○　　♿

ARRAW BRAHMA

84–43 164th Street
Jamaica, Queens
(718) 523-2600

Inexpensive vegetarian food served and prepared in an inspiring atmosphere by disciples of Sri Chinmoy. They have a large menu that changes daily. Chinese dishes are prepared on Tuesdays, Italian food on Thursdays, and so on throughout the week. The Vegetable Kabobs are delicious.

Free meditation classes are offered in the evenings and on weekends. Sri Chinmoy's books and thoughts are everywhere, and they even have a dais all set up and waiting for him in case he wanders in for coffee.

Mon., Tues. & Thurs.–Sat.: 11:00am–10:00pm
Wednesday: 11:00am–2:00pm
Sunday: 12:00pm–10:00pm
Call first to insure that they're open, as the hours fluctuate.

Inexpensive

v   ♿

APPLE RESTAURANT

17 Waverly Place
(Between Greene & Mercer Streets)
(212) 473–8888

This restaurant, which is owned by the former proprietor of Village Natural, has something for everyone. Housed in what was once "Garvin's" (a fancy French restaurant, now closed) it has a lavish interior. Its prices, however, belie the elegance of its decor. The owners show old movies on a little screen, play excellent jazz music over the sound system, and feature Karaoke (Japanese sing–along) too. Although they do have a Vietnamese meat section on their menu, they have a huge vegetarian menu as well. All of the vegetarian dishes are prepared in a separate kitchen, and most are available without dairy. Try the Crispy Seitan &

Pecans over Spinach Noodles–delish.

Monday–Thursday: 11:00am–11:00pm
Friday, Saturday: 11:00am–12:00am
Sunday: 11:00am–10:00pm

Moderate–Expensive

VF ♼ 🍸 💣✳ ♿

B & ẞ DAIRY

127 Second Avenue
(Near 8th Street)
(212) 505–8065

"Kosher style" (their description) dairy restaurant.
Good food. Low prices. Lots of atmosphere. No
meat. A gathering place for characters. They have
superb freshly baked Challah Bread, Homemade
Blintzes, Vegetable Lasagna–and more. Specials
change daily. Besides, how many other dairy restaurants can you go to on Saturday? If you're claustrophobic, though, this is probably not the best
place for you, as it's really tiny. Pay strict attention, or you'll be eating your neighbor's food by
mistake. Although they informally permit smoking, they will ask the smoker to stop if you say
something.

Seven days: 7:30am–10:00pm

Inexpensive

V

BACHUÉ

36 West 21st Street
(Between 5th & 6th Avenues)
(212) 229–0870

Totally vegan, well thought out menu with the focus on South American cuisine, Bachué (pronounced bah–chu–way) is a goddess of Colombia's Chibcha people. It's also one of the best places in New York to experience gourmet vegan cuisine. Inspired by the theories of Anne Marie Colbin from the Natural Gourmet Cooking School, they also have a vegan home delivery service called "Earth Cuisine." Bachué uses many organic ingredients, and none of the dishes have any meat, dairy products, eggs, or honey. They also serve a number of scrumptious vegan breakfasts all day long.

Monday and Tuesday: 8:00am–6:00pm
Wednesday–Friday: 8:00am–10:00pm
Saturday: 10:00am–10:00pm
Sunday: Closed

Inexpensive

Ve   O   ☯   ♿

BAMBOO GARDEN RESTAURANT

41–28 Main Street
(Near 41st Road)
Flushing, Queens
(718) 463–9240

Vegetarian Chinese restaurant in the heart of Flushing right near the subways, buses, and general hubbub. Sister restaurant of the very wonderful Vegetarian Heaven on Manhattan's Columbus Circle. This place has no meat, fish, dairy, MSG, or bad karma, man. Instead, they boast 116 varieties of mock chicken, fish, and meat dishes with eight different sauces. The "Duck" Soup is good, as is the Sesame "Chicken," which our daughter loved, as well as the Shredded "Pork" with Mustard Greens. Bamboo Garden is kosher as well. The main entrance is down a number of flights, which would make it prohibitive for anyone in a wheelchair, but the side entrance on 41st Road has only two steps.

Seven days: 11:00am–10:30pm

Moderate

v   ✡   ♿

BELL CAFÉ

310 Spring Street
(Between Greenwich and Hudson Streets)
(212) 334–BELL

Hip hangout with poetry on the walls, makeshift chairs and tables, and a crowd that's up to the minute cool. They have a good selection of veggie offerings: Vegetarian Shepherd's Pie, Non–Dairy Pizza, Tempeh Loaf, Quesadillas, and more! Monthly "art parties" the first Monday of every month. This place is a cool scene, and they're definitely accommodating to vegans.

Sunday-Thursday: 11:30pm–2:00am
Friday and Saturday: 11:30pm–4:00am

Moderate

V   &

BERRIE'S (FORMERLY CAFÉ BLOOM)

321 Amsterdam Avenue
(75th & 76th Streets)

25th Street
(Between Park & Lexington Avenues)
(212) 874–3032

High–quality, mostly vegetarian (they also serve chicken) buffet–style restaurant with a decidedly Middle–Eastern flavor. The gimmick here is their "combine any three dishes for $4.95" deal. You'll definitely feel well fed after a five–dollar plate here. The Roasted Potatoes with Garlic, Coriander, and Lemon was excellent, as was the Cauliflower with Carrots and Tahini, and the Sautéed Spinach with Garlic Sauce. In fact, everything we had was fresh and delectably seasoned.

Seven days: 11:00am–10:00pm

Inexpensive
VF

BERRY'S BURRITOS

113 Greenwich Avenue (Near Jane Street)
West Village
(212) 727–0584 (West Village)

93 Avenue A (Near 6th Street)
East Village
(212) 254–2054 (East Village)

A friend of ours from San Francisco says this place is the real McCoy. Mexican, delicious, and cheap. In fact, probably one of the best Mexican restaurants in all of New York—especially in terms of the money–to–food ratio. The quality of food is excellent, and the prices are extremely reasonable–particularly for vegetarians. Non–dairy Burritos are available, and there's often a line to get in at both locations. The East Village locale has a take–out division right next door, and the West Village locale has a take–out division across the street.

Sunday–Wednesday: 11:00am–12:00am
Thursday–Saturday: 11:00am–1:00am

Moderate

VF Y ☙ ♿

BERTHA'S

2160 Broadway
(Near 76th Street)
(212) 362–2500

Upper West Side outpost of the renowned Benny's Burritos of the East and West Village. Same menu, same vegetarian options. If you like Benny's, come here. You'll get the same high-quality vittles without the wait or the attitude.

Monday–Friday: 11:30am–11:30pm
Saturday and Sunday: 11:00am–12:30am

Inexpensive

VF

BLUE NILE

103 West 77th Street
(Near Amsterdam Avenue)
(212) 580–3232

Ethiopian restaurant on the Upper West Side offering a good selection of meatless, dairyless entrees (see Abyssinia for the lowdown on Ethiopian food). You sit around a large wicker table inside of which is placed a large tray of Injera (a Crepe–like Flatbread). Your food is served on top of it. To eat, you tear off pieces of the Injera and sop up your food with it Some vegetarian items are available. Not as good as Abyssinia downtown, and a little bit more expensive too. However, if you're uptown and you want to try some Ethiopian food, this is it.

Seven days: 5:00pm–11:00pm

Moderate

VF

BOOSTAR

5 MacDougal Street
(Near Bleecker Street)
(212) 533–9561

Mediterranean vegetarian restaurant on New York's famed MacFalafel street, serving Pasta, Steamed Veggies, some Dairy and Fish dishes, as well as lotsa things in Pita. The Vegetarian Moussaka is very good indeed, as is the Eggplant Sandwich. The Potato–Mushroom Pie was very good, and the Humous, stuffed Avocado was an innovative idea. The Couscous is well prepared, topped with lots of nice Veggies, and sweetened with Raisins, Cinnamon, and Nuts. If the weather's nice, sit outdoors and watch the beatniks. My cousin Melvin likes this place, but you know him.

Monday–Friday: 12:00pm–1:00am
Saturday and Sunday: 12:00pm–2:00am

Inexpensive

VF   **Me**

BRIGHTON BEACH DAIRY RESTAURANT

410 Brighton Beach Ave
Brighton Beach, Brooklyn

(718) 646–7421

Come to "Little Oddessa by the Sea," and discover the preponderance of local characters. The food is about a '3,' but it's all made there. While you're there, you can go to the beach, you can get bargains on Brighton Beach avenue, you can pretend you're in the Ukraine, you can visit Mrs. Stahl's Knishes.

Sunday–Thursday: 10:00am–7:45pm
Friday: 8:00am–2:00pm

Inexpensive

v   ✡   ♿

BURRITOVILLE

1489 First Avenue
(Between 77th & 78th Streets)
(212) 472–8800

141 Second Avenue
(Between 8th & 9th Streets)
(212) 260–3300

1606 Third Avenue
(Between 90th & 91st Streets)
(212) 410–2255

148 West 4th Street
(Near 6th Avenue)
(212) 505–1212

451 Amsterdam Avenue
(Near 81st & 82nd Street)

(212) 787–8181

36 Water Street
(Near Broad Street)
(212) 747–1100

The latest and greatest exciting installment in the continuing tale of the amazing, proliferating Burrito parlor. Like many other Burrito establishments around town, this joint offers the delicious, reasonably priced, meal–for–a–day we've come to expect. The Lost In Austin Burrito has Fresh Spinach, Mushrooms, Brown Rice, Cheese, Beans, Pico de Galo, and Sour Cream. We were able to substitute Soy Cheese and Tofu Sour Cream for its Bovine surrogates with no problem ($1.00 extra, though). The Vegged Out in Santa Fe Burrito is totally vegan, and has the usual stuff plus Grilled Vegetables. If you prefer a Whole Wheat to a White Flour Tortilla, you've gotta say so. Conclusion: pretty durn good, we'd say, gringo. Now, dance! Incidentally, the Water Street location has breakfast (including a great Soy Chorizo) as well as Beer and Wine (if that's your thang).

Sunday–Thursday: 11:00am–11:00pm
Friday and Saturday: 11:00am–12:00am
Monday–Saturday: 7:00am–9:00pm–Water Street

Inexpensive

VF   ♿   🍸

CAFÉ VIVA

2578 Broadway
(Near 97th Street)
(212) 663–VIVA; (800)–209–8482

Vegetarian Pizzeria and all–round Italian restaurant supreme! Many different kinds of Pizza made with casein–free Soy Cheese and Whole Wheat or Cornmeal crusts. Exceptional Vegetarian Lasagna, Ravioli, and Calzones too. The Pesto Pizza is delicious. Check it out if you if you do dairy. They also have a good variety of Salads and a Fresh Juice Bar. Also, the Aztec Pizza (with Grilled Onions, Sweet Peppers, and Corn) is out of this world! Ya gotta check this place out!

Sunday–Thursday: 11:00am–11:30pm
Friday and Saturday: 11:00am–11:30pm

Inexpensive

v &

CARAVAN OF DREAMS

405 East 6th Street
(Near 1st Avenue)
(212) 254–1613

Very comforting atmosphere, dark, exotic, and reflective. The owner, Angel, is committed to the use of organic ingredients in all the dishes. When last there, we enjoyed the Carbo Platter (Polenta with Squash Sauce and Grain of the Day) and the Banana and Carob Shake made with Almond Milk, which was quite delish. Most of the food is dairy-free and a good number of the dishes are wheat-free too. They frequently have live music in the front and various entertaining and educational programs in the back room as well. Also, part of their receipts is donated to the "Green Corps," a training school for young environmentalists.

Seven days 12:00pm-11:00pm

Moderate

Ve

CORNER CAFÉ

3552 Johnson Avenue
(Near 236th Street)
Riverdale, Bronx
(718) 601-2861

Kosher–dairy restaurant that serves Veggies, Fish, and Pastas, very well prepared with some Middle-Eastern specialties as well. They also have a bakery with excellent homemade Pastries, Cookies, Breads, Cakes, and Tarts.

Sunday–Thursday: 8:00am–9:30pm
Friday: 8:00am–2:30pm
Saturday: Closed

Inexpensive

v

DAIRY PALACE

2210 Victory Boulevard
(Near Bradley Avenue)
Staten Island
(718) 761–5200

Kosher dairy vegetarian restaurant and pizza joint
with a deceptively humble exterior. They have a
huge menu offering such sumptuous Middle-
Eastern American delicacies as "Schwarma" or
"Steak" with Fries, as well as an equally gigantic
Chinese menu offering such goodies as General
Tso's "Chicken" and Pepper "Steak." Most of the
offerings are a little heavy on the grease, but we
still felt very well fed.

Sunday–Thursday: 10:30am–8:30pm
Friday: 11:00am–2:30pm
Saturday: Sundown–12:30am

Moderate

v   ✡   ♿

DINING AT RUBI'S

Mart 125 (260 West 125th Street)
Mezzanine Level–Across from the
Apollo Theater
(212) 666–RUBI

Directly across the street from the Apollo Theater is the Mart 125 Mall. Wind your way upstairs
past a few stalls and there's Rubi's. Modestly sized
counter service with a couple of tables nearby.
Plenty of vegetarian items. Some examples are

the Vegetarian Burgers, Veggie Hot Dogs, Rainbow Vegetarian Special Sandwich (in Pita), Vegetarian "Salmon," and the "Chicken" Salad. The menu states: "For the best in tasty Afro–centric delicacies, health food for the body and soul." It's true. Catering is available and organic produce is frequently used. For wheelchair access, use the elevator in the back.

Monday and Tuesday: 10:00am–6:30pm
Wednesday–Saturday: 10:00am–7:30pm
Sunday: 12:00pm–5:00pm

Inexpensive

VF   O   &

DOCTOR SQUEEZE

4 West 23rd Street
(Near 5th Avenue)
(212) 243–5842

If juicing is your thang, and compelling evidence suggests that it should be, check this place out. Juice bar (and only juice bar) extraordinaire. Everything squeezed (or is that squozen?) on the spot, low prices, and quick service. Some specialties include the "Big Squeeze" (Carrot, Spinach, Celery, and Parsley) and the Wheatgrass "Tooter"; the "Atomic Squeeze" (Apples, Sweet Peppers, Ginger and Parsley). Many more. Hot, healthy soups in the winter. No information was available, however, on whether or not the fruits and vegetables are organic.

Monday–Friday: 8:00am–8:00pm
Possible weekend hours in the summer

Inexpensive

Ve   ☻   ♿

DOJO RESTAURANT

24 Saint Mark's Place
(Near 2nd Avenue)
(212) 674–9821

An oh so popular new agie pseudo natural Japanese slop joint in the trendy East Village where you can get a few vegetarian dishes. Try the Vegetable Tempura–it's pretty good. They also serve fish and meat—especially fish and meat with black T–shirts and mohawks. But seriously, folks... for $2.95 you can get the famous Soyburger platter (arguably the best veggie burger in New York), which comes with a nice salad and a goodly helping of brown rice. Now that's a bargain!

Monday–Friday: 11:00am–1:00am
Saturday: 11:00am–2:00am
Sunday: 11:00am–1:00am

Inexpensive

VF   💣*   ♿

DOJO (JJ)

14 West 4th Street
(Near Mercer Street)
(212) 505–8934

Similar to the East Village branch in terms of menu. For us they feature Soyburgers, Veggie Plates, Vegetable Tempura, and lots more. Soon to be a major N.Y.U. hangout. The Japanese Brunch, which comes with Miso and a Salad, and which is served until 5:00pm, offers an option of Steamed Broccoli with Tofu Sauce over Brown Rice. Don't forget the $2.95 Soyburger platter, kiddies (Soyburger over Brown Rice with Tahini Dressing and a Salad)! It's a bargain!

Sunday–Thursday: 11:00am–1:00am
Friday, Saturday: 11:00am–2:00am

Inexpensive

VF &

EDER ROCK

2325 Broadway
(Between 84th & 85th Streets)
(212) 873–1361

Lebanese restaurant. For us they serve–Tabouli, Baba Ghanoush, Lentils and Rice, and the usual Middle–Eastern fare. However, the quality is above average. Try the Vegetable Pie or the Bamia (Fried Okra with Tomatoes, Onions, and Middle–Eastern Spices).

Seven days: 9:00am–12:00am

Inexpensive
VF

ERI'S CAFÉ

347 East 61st Street
(Between 1st and 2nd Avenues)
(212) 421–6436

Cozy little macrobiotic Japanese–style restaurant in the shadow of the 59th Street Bridge (slow down, ya move too fast...) that uses organically grown produce and has a vast selection for our ilk. Try the Futomaki (Carrot, Cucumber, Avocado, and Shiitake Mushrooms), or the Tempeh Croquette. Before or after your meal, take a ride on the Roosevelt Island Tramway, which will cost you a subway token and is one of the best cheap thrills in N.Y.

Monday–Saturday: 5:00pm–10:00pm
Sunday: Closed

Moderate

Ve   ☯   O

EVA'S

11 West 8th Street
(Between 5th and 6th Avenues)
(212) 677–3496

Middle–Eastern fast–food style restaurant with a broad selection of Vegetarian Salads and Sandwiches (Falafel, Baba Ghanoush, Vine Leaves with Brown Rice, Baked Tofu, and more). They also feature Nature Burgers (Brown Rice, Sunflower Seeds, Herbs, Spices) and Veggie Nuggets (was that the sound of Ray Kroc spinning in his grave?)

Although they do serve some meat and fish items, the bulk of the menu is vegetarian and quite good. An ongoing deal here is that if you buy the special sandwich of the day, they give you another one for $1.50—not bad. In addition, there's a well-stocked natural foods store in the back, and the entire restaurant is smoke–free.

Seven days: 10:00am–11:30pm

Inexpensive

VF　　♿

EVERYTHING NATURAL

3810 White Plains Road
(Between 219th and 220th Streets)
Da Bronx
(718) 652–9070

West–Indian take–out restaurant with a good selection of hot vegetarian food sold by the plate. A small plate is $4.00, a medium plate is $6.00, and a large plate is $8.00. You choose the size you want and tell them which goodies to include. Some options include Vegetarian "Duck" with Okra and White Beans (delicious, but we believe it contains MSG), Coconut Rice and Peas, and Seasoned Potatoes. They feature a fairly well–stocked natural foods store as well. Their menu states "Jah annointeth our heads with oil, our blenders runneth over."

Monday–Saturday: 8:00am–11:00pm
Sunday: 9:00am–9:00pm

Inexpensive

Ve &

EVERYTHING VITAL

300 Troy Avenue (South of Eastern Parkway)
Crown Heights, Brooklyn
(718) 953–9433

The Brooklyn branch of Everything Natural. Totally vegan, Caribbean, and delicious. This is a take-out place (no seating) that our opinions diverge on, especially regarding one particular dish: the Veggie "Duck." It's made from Curried Tofu Skins and comes with Lima Beans and Sweet Red Peppers. One of us loves it, and one of us swears it contains MSG. Hey, it's just like Siskel and Ebert in this book. The Bulgur was great, and fresh juices are offered as well. The Apple and Carrot mixture is recommended. The Sweet Potato Pudding will satisfy your sweet tooth, or for the ultimate sugar high, buy a piece of fresh Sugar Cane—chopped and peeled before your eyes. Nice decorations here too.

Seven days: 7:30am–10:00pm

Inexpensive

Ve &

FAMOUS PITA

935 Coney Island Avenue
(Between Ditmas & Newkirk Avenues)

Kensington, Brooklyn
(718) 282–0868

Israeli–Yemenite falafel joint supreme. Everything is made on premises, including the Pita bread, which you can frequently watch being baked in the back of the restaurant. "Hey, help yourself to our salad bar." The idea is to get a $3.00 sandwich and then pile $6.00 worth of salad bar stuff on it–that's how it's done at Falafel stands in Israel. Don't miss the Roasted Eggplant at the end of the bar. Try the Malawach as well. It's a chewy dough dish from Yemen. Fresh hot soups are available as well—usually a Vegetable soup and a Bean Soup. Make sure you try the Amba Sauce on your Falafel. It's a tart, Iraqi–Indian specialty made with a delicious Mango base. Although they do have that 'turkey–on–a–spit–thing' in the front window, Famous Pita is the best example of a "Falafel with an all–you–can–pile–on–salad–bar" emporium in New York.

Monday–Thursday: 8:00am–3:00am
Friday: 8:00am–4:00pm
Saturday: Closed
Sunday: 8:00am–3:00pm

Inexpensive

VF   ✡   ♿

FREDDIE AND PEPPER'S GOURMET PIZZERIA

303 Amsterdam Avenue
(Between 74th & 75th Streets)
(212) 799–BEST

Deceptively standard–looking pizzeria with a couple of quite notable exceptions: you can get just about any vegetable as a topping, Whole Wheat Pizza, and freshly baked Soy Cheese Pizza. The cheese used on this is a product called Soya melt, which the owners say is totally without dairy. It's pretty good, so we have our suspicions, but that's what they say. The decor and ambiance are easily as scuzzy as any N.Y. pizzeria, but would you rather have the pristine, ketchup–covered cardboard of a Pizza Hut? Anyway, Domino's funds the right–to–life movement.

Sunday–Thursday: 11:00am–11:30pm
Friday and Saturday: 11:00am–3:00am

Inexpensive
VF

GOOD FOOD CAFÉ

401 5th Avenue
(Near 38th Street)
(212) 686–3546

This place is a find. Cute little café near the Empire State Building with a nice selection and reasonable prices. The Tofu–Mushroom Casserole with Brown Rice and Sprouts is fantastic. You get a huge portion for only $5.40. Although some fish and chicken are sold, there is a wonderfully large vegetarian menu and a very nice atmosphere. Specials change daily.

Monday–Friday: 11:30am–7:00pm
Saturday: 12:0pm–5:00pm
Sunday: Closed

Inexpensive

VF   ♿

GOOD ḤEALTḤ CAFÉ
324 East 86th Street
(Between 1st & 2nd Avenues)
(212) 439–9680

The Whole Wheat Dumplings served with an array of Steamed Vegetables and Tamari Ginger Sauce was a light, exquisite meal. A companion had the Macro Plate: Hijiki, Black–eyed Peas (which was the bean of the day), Brown Rice, and Steamed Vegetables. The desserts are good—the Blueberry-Peach Pie, for example, was super. Like its companion restaurants Quantum Leap and Village Natural, there are always daily specials and a casserole of the day. Also, there's a well–stocked natural foods store inside.

Monday–Thursday: 11:30am–10:00pm
Friday: 11:30am–11:00pm
Saturday and Sunday: 10:00am–10:00pm

Moderate

v   ♿

GOURMET CAFÉ

1622 Coney Island Avenue
(Between Avenues L & M)
Midwood, Brooklyn
(718) 338–5825

Kosher vegetarian dairy restaurant/café in the heart of Midwood providing high–quality vittles to the community. Plenty of meat substitutes are available, such as Vegetarian Hungarian Goulash, Bombay "Chicken," "Chicken" Nuggets and Vegetarian "Goulash." They also have some very nice frozen meals to take home and a line of delicious muffins. Some of the side dishes, however, are not always at their freshest.

Monday–Thursday: 11:30am–10:00pm
Friday and Saturday: Closed
Sunday: 12:30pm–10:00pm

Moderate

v   ✡   ♿

GOVINDA'S

In front of 80 Broadway
(Near Wall Street)

Cute little pushcart located in front of 80 Broadway at the corner of Wall Street. (A mere stone's throw from the Stock Exchange) with picture of various Hindu deities adorning the awning. Try the Veggie Burger, which is served in Pita and is fantastic (especially for the price), the Vegetarian Chili, or soup. Freshly squeezed juices are available as well, along with various seasonal treats. Buy low, sell high.

Seasonally, Monday–Friday: 11:00am–3:00pm

Inexpensive

V   &

GREAT AMERICAN HEALTH BAR

2 Park Avenue
(Between 32nd & 33rd Streets)

35 West 57th Street
(Between 5th & 6th Avenues)

821 3rd Avenue
(Near 50th Street)

Manhattan (all 212)
685–7117–2 Park Avenue
355–5177–35 West 57th Street
758–0883–821 Third Avenue

These places are great! Styled after 1940's lunch counters, they're a vegetarian's answer to McD*nl*d's. Soup, Sandwiches, Salads and fresh juices—all natural, mostly vegetarian, and in a few locations. All three sites are Kosher and except for the one on West 57th Street, wheelchair accessible.

2 Park Avenue:
Monday–Wednesday: 7:00am–7:00pm
Thursday: 7:00am–8:00pm

Friday: 7:00am–3:00pm
Saturday & Sunday: Closed

35 West 57th Street:
Seven days: 8:00am–10:00pm

821 Third Avenue:
Monday–Friday: 7:30am–8:00pm
Saturday & Sunday: 11:00am–8:00pm

Moderate

V ✡

ḦARRY'S BURRITOS

91 East 7th Street
(Between Avenue A & 1st Avenue)
(212) 477–0773

Similar to Benny's Burritos on 6th Street (good, cheap Mexican vittles), except this place is more for take–out. Benny's, Harry's, and Healthy Henrrietta's in Brooklyn were once owned by three partners who have since consolidated their efforts toward Benny's. Excellent quality at all three places.

Seven days: 12:00pm–1:00am

Inexpensive

VF ♿

HEALTH PUB

371 Second Avenue
(Near 21st Street)
(212) 529-9200

Upscale, nearly vegan restaurant in Gramercy Park (none of the food is made with meat, eggs, dairy products, or sugar, however, they do serve fish) with an extremely high–quality menu. Some available goodies are Marinated Grilled Tofu, Golden Cornbread with Amaranth, Oriental Stirfry, and Blackbean Chili. The Seitan Marsala with Brown Rice and Kale was superb, and for dessert, the Almond Pudding with Cherry Sauce was the best thing we've had in our mouths since weaning. If you feel like boozing it up, they serve organic wines. You've never really had good wine until you've had some made from unsprayed grapes with no chemical additives. The Hazelnut Carob Torte with Raspberry Topping is exquisite as well. Leave them fishies in the sea, though.

Seven days: 11:00am–11:00pm
Kitchen closes at 10:30pm

Expensive

Ve

HEALTHFUL ESSENCE

Liberty Street
(Between Broadway and Church Street)

About ten feet away from the little park that has

the statue of the businessman looking through his briefcase is the Healthful Essence Pushcart. Your hostess, Princess, at this al fresco experience offers some delicious examples of vegetarian West Indian fare. Try the Vegetarian Rotis, the Veggie Patties, or the Peanut Stew.

Seasonally, Monday–Friday: 11:00am–3:00pm

Inexpensive

v   &

ŊEALŦŊY CAŊDLE

972 Lexington Avenue
(Near 71st Street)
(212) 472–0970

Vegetarian fast food restaurant offering take–out and delivery only. Their core constituency is the Hunter College and Upper East Side crowds, and they claim to be one of the first juice bars in N.Y. Try the soups (which change daily), the Macro Plate, and/or the Vegetarian Chili. Quality is quite high and the selection is quite ample.

Monday–Friday: 7:30am–7:45pm
Saturday: 7:30am–5:00pm
Sundays: Closed

Moderate

Ve   ☯

HEALTHY CANDLE (CANDLE CAFÉ)

1307 Third Avenue
(Near 75th Street)
(212) 472–0970

One of the oldest and finest juice bars and natural food shacks in N.Y. is finally opening a place where you can sit down and have a meal. Scheduled to debut in the summer of 1994, they'll be able to seat 50 people, and will offer the same macro goodies that have made Healthy Candle famous for over 40 years.

Hours not available at press time.

Moderate

Ve   ☯

HEALTHY CHELSEA

248 West 23rd Street
(Near 8th Avenue)
(212) 691–0286

Take–out health food store and juice bar with a small vegetarian steam table. By the end of the day some of the entrees in their steam table look a bit ragged, so go early. Some sandwiches and shakes are available as well. Stop into the Chelsea Hotel while you're there and ask if Sid and Nancy have been in.

Monday–Saturday: 10:00am–10:00pm
Sunday: 12:00pm–9:00pm

Inexpensive

V   &

ḤEꞀLꞭꞭY ḤEꞀꞀꞀJEꞭꞀ'S

60 Henry Street
(Between Cranberry & Orange Streets)
Brooklyn Heights, Brooklyn
(718) 858–8478

Wonderful high–quality vegetarian Macrobiotic
Mexican restaurant located in Brooklyn Heights.
You can choose Regular or Tofu Sour Cream on
your Burrito, and you have your choice of Beans
(Black, Pinto, or Aduki) and Rice (Yellow and
Brown). They use Organic Beans and Grains and
Filtered Water. All the food is muy deliciosos.
Also, the owners are very nice.

Seven days: 11:00am–11:00pm

Inexpensive

Ve   &

ḤEꞀLꞭꞭY ḤEꞀꞀꞀJEꞭꞀ'S ON ꞭḤE SLOPE

787 Union Street
(Near 6th Avenue)
Park Slope, Brooklyn
(718) 622–2924

Same basic menu and decor as the flagship branch
in Brooklyn Heights—Macrobiotic Mexican yum-
yums. Brilliant choice of location this—1/2 block

47

from the Park Slope Food Coop. They always
have a great selection of specials, and everything
(and we mean everything) is broken down by ingredients.

Seven days: 11:00am–11:00pm

Inexpensive

Ve   &

ꞪEALTꞪY PLEASURES

93 University Place
(Near 11th Street)
(212) 353-FOOD

One of the newest and finest natural food super-
markets; besides a wide selection of grocery type
things, they offer a great deli take-out section
(with goodies such as Sauteed Seitan and Curried
Tempeh).

Seven days: 7:00am-10:00pm

Prices vary

VF &

ꞪORG KORG VEGETARIAR

1400 2nd Avenue
(Between 72nd & 73rd Streets)
(212) 472–8717 or 8749

The new kid on the block, a welcome addition to

the Upper East Side. Vegetarian Chinese, if you couldn't guess. Totally vegan, good selection. Try the Stir Fried Rainbow "Eel" or the "Scallops" Szechuan Style. Affiliated with the renowned "House of Vegetarian" restaurant in Chinatown.

Monday–Saturday: 12:00pm–11:00pm
Sunday and Holidays: 1:00pm–11:00pm

Moderate–Expensive

Ve   ♿

HOUSE OF FALAFEL VEGETARIAN STYLE

620 Nostrand Avenue
(Between Dean & Pacific Streets)
Bedford-Stuyvesant, Brooklyn
(718) 735–0009

Very nice take-out place with a little counter. They have a different menu for every day of the week. The Macaroni Pie is like a Casserole stuffed with Veggies. Delicious. The Callaloo is like Creamed Spinach with Coconut and West Indian spices. And of course, the Falafel with the "works" (which, as one might imagine, is their specialty) is simply great.

Monday–Saturday: 10:00am–8:30pm
Sunday: Closed

Inexpensive

V   ♿

ȠOUSE OF VEGETARIAN

68 Mott Street
(Between Canal & Bayard Streets)
(212) 226–6572

Vegetarian Chinese Restaurant on Chinatown's main street offering very good fare at quite reasonable prices. We especially like the Lemon "Chicken" and the Iron "Steak" (both made from White Yams). The Mock "Ham" was seasoned just right. For your appetizer, try the assorted Gluten and/or the Gluten "Duck" (they're both delicious) or the Spring Rolls, which are a bit greasy. But who knows, maybe you like that.

Seven days: 11:00am–11:00pm

Moderate–Expensive

Ve

ȠUNAN DELIGȠT

752 Union Street
(Near 6th Avenue)
Park Slope, Brooklyn
(718) 789–1400; 1415

The menu says "In accordance with traditional Buddhist/Vegan practice, all our dishes are prepared entirely with vegetables and vegetable derivatives." However, we learned that eggwhites are used and they also have another menu for meat-eaters. The Corn and Fresh Mushroom Soup is great. It's thick, sort of like a porridge. The Steamed Vegetable Dumplings are a little bland, but the Steamed Spinach Dumplings are delicious. The Spicy Sesame "Chicken" is amazing (if a bit on the sweet side), and the Taro "Chicken" a la King" is extraordinary, with Fresh Vegetables, a Crispy Taro Root Crust, and a Savory Sauce. A great place to eat after working or shopping at the Park Slope Food Coop. They have a full menu of lunch specials but none of their veggie entrees are on that menu. They need a little encouragement.

Monday–Thursday: 11:30am–10:30pm
Friday and Saturday: 11:30am–11:30pm
Sunday: 1:00pm–10:30pm

Moderate

V

INDIAN DELHI

392 Columbus Avenue
(Near 79th Street)
(212) 362–8760

This used to be the Indian Kitchen (on 78th and Broadway), which was too wonderful for words. Then the all–too–common "landlord problems" intervened and they had to move. Like its former incarnation, they serve great Vegetarian Indian food in a spiritual atmosphere. Try the "Indian Falafel" (Chickpeas, Cabbage, and Salad wrapped up in a flat Pita topped with Onion Relish)–a bargain, or get a Vegetable Combo Plate with your choice of any three Veggies over Rice (another bargain, especially considering the quality). We are sad to note that as of press time, this long–standing strictly vegetarian establishment has begun serving chicken and fish!! We hope that by the next edition they will have reconsidered.

Monday–Saturday: 11:00am–11:00pm
Sunday: 11:00am–11:00pm

Inexpensive
VF   &

INTEGRAL YOGA

299 West 13th Street
(Between 7th and 8th Avenues)
(212) 243–2642

Extremely well-stocked natural food store with a little something extra in the back. That "something extra" is one of the best take–out salad–bars and steam–tables in the city. Some items from the steam table include Tofu Ravioli, Bok Choy and Tofu, Lemon Tempeh, and more. Some of the Sandwiches they offer include their "Faloney" Sandwich and their Mock Tuna. They also offer wonderful vegetarian cooking classes available through its bookstore next door.

Monday–Friday: 10:00am–9:30pm
Saturday: 10:00am–8:30pm
Sunday: 12:00pm–6:30pm

Inexpensive

Ve   O

J RANKIN' ITAL STOP

804 Nostrand Avenue
(Between St. John's & Lincoln Places)
Crown Heights, Brooklyn
(718) 467–7630

All praise to His Majesty Haile Selassie I. All the food here is strictly "Ital," which means "no flesh is served." The Veggie Pattie has a Gram Burger filling (Gram Burger is a West Indian meat substitute sort of like T.V.P.) and a Coconut tasting dough—it's delicious. There are a few tables and a long counter; you get your food from the counter and sit down or take it out. Fresh breads and cakes are available as well.

Monday–Saturday: 9:00am–10:00pm
Sunday: Closed

Inexpensive

Ve   &

JOSEPHINA

1900 Broadway
(Near Lincoln Center)
(212) 799–1000

Sophisticated natural foods restaurants offering quite a bit for vegans and vegetarians. Organically raised produce is frequently used, and most of the entrees are dairy free. Try the Protein Plate (Quinoa, Wheat Berries, and a Vegetable Tortilla). Fills in the gap around Lincoln Center. If you're eating here before the theater, reservations are suggested; otherwise just mosey on in.

Monday–Friday: 12:00pm–12:00am
Saturday: 11:30am–12:00am
Sunday: 11:30am–12:00am

Expensive

VF　　Y　　O　　&

JOSIE'S

300 Amsterdam Avenue
(Near 74th Street)
(212) 769-1212

Like their sister restaurant Josephina, Josie's *raison d'être* (that means *raisins on a tray*) is to provide high-quality, well-prepared, natural cuisine and thus change your mind about how good natural food can be. We'll drink to that! While their committment to meatless cuisine is quite good (that's why you're reading about them in our book) Josie's is a viable option for a mixed (veggies and carnies) group, as they have many of the American "standards" as well.

Sunday and Tuesday–Thursday: 5:00pm–10:30pm

Friday and Saturday: 5:00pm–12:00am

Moderate

VF 🍸 O ♿

KAR

5908 Avenue N
(Near Ralph Ave)
Mill Basin, Brooklyn
(718) 531–8811

2212 Avenue X
(Between East 22nd & East 23rd Streets)
Sheepshead Bay, Brooklyn
(718) 891–6868 (Take–out only)

Superb Chinese restaurants with an emphasis on low salt, low fat, fresh, healthy food. Brown rice is available, and they don't use MSG either. Service is always exceptional, and the food is always superb. The interesting thing about Kar is that they have different specials at each branch. Try the Whole Wheat Vegetable Dumplings for an appetizer or the Baby Eggplant with Garlic Sauce. The Crispy Tofu Pot is scrumptious.

Monday–Thursday: 12:00pm–10:30pm
Friday and Saturday: 12:00pm–11:30pm

Monday–Thursday: 11:30am–10:00pm
Friday and Saturday: 1:00pm–11:30pm

Moderate

VF &

KAR LUK

437 Fifth Avenue
(Near 9th Street)
Park Slope, Brooklyn
(718) 832–4500

To all outward appearances, your standard Chinese take–out with a few tables. However, Kar–Luck is run by the former first chef of the now closed Kar of Park Slope (a wonderful, health-oriented Chinese restaurant on 5th Avenue). They offer an extensive vegetarian menu and in particular the Vegetarian Sesame Chicken is excellent. The Vegetarian Hot and Sour Soup is a little too salty, though.

Monday–Thursday: 11:30am–10:30pm
Friday and Saturday: 11:30am–11:30pm
Sunday: 12:30pm–10:30pm

Inexpensive

VF &

KINGS VEGETARIAN RESTAURANT

4705 Church Avenue
(Near East 47th Street)

East Flatbush, Brooklyn
(718) 284-4533

Excellent Rastafarian vegetarian restaurant in East Flatbush. Of note are the Whole Wheat, freshly baked Veggie Patties—spicy. The Rice and Peas are good, if a little bland, as are the greens, but the Red Peas and Pumpkin is good. Primarily for take–out, however, they have two tables so you can sit down if you choose. They also serve fish. Nice people, generally good food, and extremely reasonable prices. However, the last few times we've eaten here, the food quality hasn't been up to par.

Seven days: 7:00am–9:00pm

Inexpensive

VF　　&

KRISH ROSH

101–02 Queens Boulevard
(Near 67th Road)
Forest Hills, Queens
(718) 897-5554

145 4th Avenue
(Between 13th & 14th Streets)
(212) 529-4910

Longtime Queens mainstay, this fine kosher knishery has no meat of course (consistent with kosher law) and offers such goodies as Spinach, Broccoli, Kasha, Carrot, and the more familiar Potato Knishes, all made on the premises. Also note the location in Manhattan.

Monday and Saturday: 9:00am–7:00pm
Tuesday–Friday: 9:00am–7:30pm
Sunday: 9:00am–6:00pm

Inexpensive

v   ✡   ♿

KOSHER CORNER

73–01 Main Street
(Near 73rd Avenue)
Kew Garden Hills, Queens
(718) 263–1177

Kosher Dairy sit–down restaurant in the ortho-
dox Jewish community centering around Main
Street and Jewel Avenue. The Vegetable Cutlet
with Mushroom Sauce was very good, and they
have a children's menu. The French Onion Soup
was pretty good too.

Sunday–Thursday: 7:30am–10:00pm
Friday: 7:30am–2:00pm
Saturday: Closed

Moderate

v   ✡   ☺   ♿

LE POEME

14 Prince Street
(Near Elizabeth Street)
(212) 941–1106

Friendly, laid back Corsican restaurant in the netherland that is the junction of Little Italy, Soho, and the Lower East Side. All the food is reasonably priced and fresher than fresh. We started with the Three Dip Plat du Jour, the dips in question being: Eggplant, Humous, and Tapenade (Black Olives and Garlic) served with the most wonderful homemade Whole Wheat Bread (which can be taken home for $4.00 a loaf—worth it). The Vegetable Lasagna was supposedly vegan (it had no visible signs of cheese or eggs, but our suspicion lingers). Nonetheless, it was delicious.

Seven Days: 8:30am–11:00pm

Moderate

VF   ♿

LENOX AVENUE HEALTH FOOD RESTAURANT

471 Lenox Avenue (A.K.A. Malcolm X Blvd.)
Between 133rd &134th Streets)
(212) 368–7663

Rastafarian vegetarian restaurant. Lunch specials are served from 11:00am to 3:00pm, which allow you to choose any three items for $5.00, or you can get any two items with the Vegetarian Lasagna, which is fantastic. Try the vegetarian "Scallops" or the Callaloo (hey, that's us). They have an incredible selection for breakfast as well—the scrambled Tofu with a side of Plantains is particularly good. Menus change daily. On your way over, check out the African bazaar on Lenox

Avenue between 125th and 128th Streets.

Monday–Saturday 7:00am–8:00pm
Sunday: Closed

Inexpensive

V &

LIFE CAFE

343 East 10th Street
(Near Avenue B)
(212) 477–9001

Artsy little café with lots and lots of vegan and
vegetarian items, such as the Mega Burrito (made
with Seitan), the Seitan Steak Sandwich, (meatless version of the "Philly Steak Sandwich) a whole
bunch of Soy drinks, and much more. Once an East
Village "performance space" (bongos and berets,
daddy–o), the name developed from the old "Life"
magazine covers that the owners put in the win-
dows of the original space to cover up the holes. A
great place to hang out with friends, drink coffee
or beer, and debate the nature of the universe.

Monday–Thursday: 12:00pm–12:00am
Friday: 12:00pm–2:00am
Saturday: 11:00am–2:00am
Sunday: 11:00am–12:00am

Moderate

VF

LIVETH'S DELIGHT VEGETARIAN RESTAURANT

1358 Saint John's Place
Weeksville, Brooklyn
(718) 735-4008

Vegetarian take-out counter/restaurant near Weeksville (one of the oldest African-American neighborhoods in NYC). The Lo-Mein was good and fresh, but the Mixed Vegetables were kind of old and dried up. The Bean dishes we sampled, made variously with Cow-peas, Chic-peas and Red-peas were quite delicious, though. The Macaroni Pie and the Gran Burgers were great as well.

Monday–Saturday: 11:30am–9:30pm

Inexpensive

v   ♿

LUMA

200 Ninth Avenue
(Between 22nd & 23rd Streets)
(212) 633–8033

Elegant "Continental-style" "natural" restaurant in Chelsea. Favored watering hole of the "hoi poloi." Try the Tempeh Scallopini or the Pumpkin Ravioli. Fish and free-range chicken (just because they've run around a little and lived the good life doesn't mean you should chop their heads off) are also served. Organic produce and grains are used, and they have a different special every night.

Fancy–schmancy. Don't ever call them a Vegetarian Restaurant though. They get quite offended by the term, and take great pains to distance themselves. Hrrumph!

Monday–Saturday: 5:30pm–10:30pm
Sunday: 5:00pm–10:00pm

Expensive

VF   **O**   ♿

ꟽꟙDRꟘꟅ ꟽꟘꟅꟘL

104 Lexington Avenue
(Between 27th & 28th Streets)
(212) 684–4010

Exceptional Indian Kosher Vegetarian restaurant on the site of what was once the justifiably renowned Madras Palace. (We feel that the quality and variety of food far surpasses that of the former occupant). They offer vegetarian dishes from all over India, not just from the Southern provinces, like many other vegetarian Indian places. The Mixed Vegetable Uthappam (a Pancake made out of Rice and Lentil Flour) was delicious. So was the Masala Dosai (resembles a gigantic Crepe). In all, we had a sumptuous repast worthy of the Vedic gods.

Seven days: 11:30am–3:00pm, 5:00pm–10:00pm

Moderate

v   ☺

MAIN EVENT

3708 Riverdale Avenue
Riverdale, Bronx
(212) 601–3013

Kosher Dairy Pizza/Falafel joint in Da Bronx.
They serve Blintzes, Vegetarian Chopped Liver,
Vegetable Cutlets, and more. They've just moved
to more palatial digs a few doors down from their
former location. This is the Riverdale hangout
where Archie, Veronica and Jughead really go—
not Pop Tate's (that's not a crown Jughead's wear-
ing—it's a yarmulke. Archie and Veronica, on the
other hand, are assimilated).

Seven days: 11:00am–9:00pm

Moderate

v   ✡   ♿

MANA

2444 Broadway
(Between 90th and 91st Streets)
(212) 787–1110

This is the site of the original Souen's, which was
quite a hit when it opened. Mana has the same
delicious cuisine, and the same high standards (no
sugar, chemicals, or dairy products). They do
serve fish, however. Quality, Japanese–style,
macrobiotic food at fairly reasonable prices. Try
the Seitan Sukiyaki. Yum, yum, eat 'em up.

Monday–Saturday: 11:30am–11:00pm
Sunday: 12:00pm–10:00pm
Moderate

Ve   ☺   ♿

MATHILDA'S BAKERY (A.K.A. ROGER'S FAMOUS MUFFINS)

1321 Ave J
(At East 14th Street)
Midwood, Brooklyn
(718) 951–8148

Kosher dairy bakery and catering. Very nice people. Delicious baked goods all made on the premises, such as Borekas (an Israeli staple—phylo dough triangles filled with Spinach, Potato, or Cheese) and a huge assortment of cakes, cookies, and other goodies, many of which are made with little or no salt or sugar. You can get Baba Ghanoush or a number of other salads on a bagel or in a platter, and they also make special holiday items like Hanukkah Jelly Doughnuts and Latkes. Their pride and joy, however, are their Muffins. Some of the spreads and salads that don't turn over so quickly may not be that fresh, so watch out. Baked goods are a better bet here.

Sunday–Thursday: 7:00am–8:00pm
Friday: 7:00am–Sundown
Saturday: Closed
Inexpensive

VF   ✡   ♿

MAVALI PALACE

46 East 29th Street
(Between Park and Madison Avenues)
(212) 679-5535

South Indian vegetarian restaurant extraordinaire! Elegant decor, wonderful atmosphere, great prices. They're still relatively new, so the staff is helpful and eager to please. There are certain restaurants in which you can sense that highly-evolved, passionate artists are at work—Mavali Palace is one. Omitting the dairy products in any dish is not a problem, so they're definitly vegan-friendly. The Chickpea Masala is exquisite as is the Iddly, and the menu goes on and on. Many feel that this is among the best Indian food available in NYC. We heartily agree.

Tuesday–Sunday: 12:00pm–10:00pm
Monday: Closed
Moderate

V

MELANIE'S NATURAL CAFÉ

445 Sixth Avenue
(Near 10th Street)
(212) 463-7744

Again that word–"Natural"! What does it mean? Close to the earth? Back to the land? No pesticides or preservatives? What?? Melanie's is a cafeteria–style joint in the heart of the West Village.

The staff is courteous and helpful, and there are separate smoking and nonsmoking areas. As for food, there are quite a few salads and vegetarian entrees. The Cajun Spiced Tofu Salad with Brown Rice and Veggies is pretty good. The staff is a bit unaware regarding the dietary needs of vegans, though. Go there and make them change that. While you're there, seat yourself by the window looking onto Sixth Avenue, and people-watch.

Monday–Friday: 8:00am–10:00pm
Saturday: 9:00am–10:00pm
Sunday: 11:00am–10:00pm
Inexpensive

VF

MICHAEL & ZOË'S (FORMERLY BROWNIE POINTS)

101 2nd Avenue
(Between 5th & 6th Streets)
(212) 254–5004

Snappy little joint that specializes, as the former name implies, in homemade Brownies (many of which are natural and vegan). They also have a very nice menu offering quite a few vegetarian entrees. For example, in the sandwich department they have Vegetarian Chicken Salad, Sunshine Burgers, Veggie Burgers, and more. They have a very good Vegetarian Cashew Chili too. Try the "Lorraine's Own," which is a mixture of Brown Rice, Wild Rice, and assorted vegetables. And don't forget a Brownie.

Sunday–Thursday: 8:00am–11:00pm
Friday and Saturday: 8:00am–1:0pm

Moderate

VF   &

MIZRACHI KOSHER PIZZA AND FALAFEL

105 Chambers Street
(Near Church Street)
(212) 964–2280

One of many kosher Israeli dairy joints in N.Y., this one boasting a fairly large selection at quite reasonable prices. Some examples include: Vegetable Lasagna, Vegetable Cutlets, Stuffed Peppers, and of course Pizza and Falafel. A good place to eat when you're subpoenaed to appear in federal court on racketeering charges.

Monday–Thursday: 7:00am–7:00pm
Friday: 7:00am–2 hrs before sunset
Saturday and Sunday: Closed

Inexpensive

V   ✡

MOUSTACHE

405 Atlantic Avenue
(Between Bond & Nevins Streets)
Boerum Hill, Brooklyn

(718) 852–5555

A Mid-Eastern "Pitza" at $5.00 is a 10–inch diameter, custom–made heapin' helpin' you won't soon forget. For a mere $1.00 extra per ingredient, you can adorn your pie with varied victuals such as Mushrooms, Olives, Eggplant, Capers, Onions, and Spinach, or our personal favorites–Garlic and Parsley. Also available are some very nice Salads and the usual Humous, Baba Ghanoush, and Falafel.

Seven days: 11:00am–11:00pm

Inexpensive

VF &

MOUSTACHE (MANHATTAN)

90 Bedford Street
(Between Grove & Barrow Streets)
(212) 229–2220

Located in Yupdom Ground Zero (where a foreign air force would drop a nuclear device to annihilate all the yuppies), Moustache's major claim to fame is its "Pitzas." The Sun-dried Tomato and Fresh Mozzarella Pitza was acceptable (a little less melting on the cheese would be desirable would be desireable). A good vegan offering is the Zatter Bread Pita with Olive Oil and Fresh Thyme. The Baba Ghanoush is good and garlicky, and they offer a Middle-Eastern Citrus drink called "Loomi" that tastes like camel piss (but one of us loved it).

Seven Days: 12:00pm–12:00am

Moderate

VF   &

MR. FALAFEL

226 7th Avenue
(Between 3rd & 4th Streets)
Park Slope, Brooklyn
(718) 768–4961

Congenial Egyptian restaurant and take–out in Park Slope serving many of the choices you might expect from Middle–Eastern cuisine. However, the food is prepared with great care, and special attention is given to providing quite a few choices for their vegetarian clientele. Falafel, Baba Ghanoush, Humous, Foul Moodamas (Fava Beans [(anybody see "Silence of the Lambs"?)] with Lemon Juice, Garlic, and Olive Oil), Egyptian Potato Salad, and more. Stop in and say hello to the Missus. Incidentally, the owner's name is Aladdin, and he will grant your every culinary wish.

Seven days: 11:00am–10:30pm

Inexpensive

VF   &

MRS. STAHL'S KNISHES

1001 Brighton Beach Avenue
(Entrance on Coney Island Avenue)

Brighton Beach, Brooklyn
(718) 648–0210

A million and one knishes. Well, perhaps we're exaggerating a bit. You've probably had a Potato Knish, maybe even a Kasha Knish somewhere along the line, but have you ever had a Cabbage, a Sweet Potato, a Potato and Mushroom, or how about a Spanish Rice Knish? Hmmm? The list goes on like you wouldn't believe. Everything here is made by hand, and you can taste it. Get a dozen assorted, walk two blocks to the ocean, and enjoy. And yes Virginia, there once was a Mrs. Stahl, who started out by peddling knishes on the board-walk during the Depression.

Thursday–Tuesday: 8:00am–7:00pm
Wednesday: 10:00am–7:00pm

Inexpensive

VF   &

NATURAL FOOD BAR

166 West 72nd Street
(Between Broadway & Amsterdam Avenue)
(212) 874–1213

Teeny–tiny–itsy–bitsy–claustrophobic little place with a big, big, super–big menu. They have Sand-wiches (the Vegetarian Chicken Salad is delicious), Salads, Soups, Juices, and more. They make Vege-tarian Eggrolls, Veggie Patties, and a Vegetarian "Cheeseburger" that's fantastic. The Homemade Cakes are great too.

Monday–Saturday: 8:00am–12:00am
Sunday: 12:00pm–10:00pm

Inexpensive

V

NATURWORKS

200A West 44th Street
(Between Broadway & 8th Avenue)
(212) 869–8335

Snappy little joint in the heart of the Theater District serving "clapboard–on–the–wall–style" cuisine that leans towards the healthy, including Salads, Veggie Burgers, Falafels, Soups, and more. Tasty, high– quality morsels with a respectable ratio of bite for the buck. Great location. It's good to know that after you've dropped $200 on Les Miz or Miss Saigon (ooh, a real helicopter!) you can still get something to eat with what's left in your pocket.

Monday–Saturday: 10:00am–9:00pm
Sunday: Closed

Inexpensive

V   &

COSMO KING

54 Varick Street
(Near Canal Street)

(212) 966–1239

Large selection of cigarettes and cigars available in the lobby. Only kidding—check out the title. But seriously, elegant, upscale restaurant in Tribeca. You might call it "Nouvelle Cuisine"—we call it "Old–velle Ripoff." Not vegetarian by a long shot–they serve chicken, fish, and rabbit! However, the food is "natural" with an emphasis on organic, and there are quite a few items for vegetarians. Some examples are Swiss Chard Polenta, Roasted Root Vegetables, and Spinach Lasagna. Good selection of "organic" wines too.

Dinner:
Monday–Thursday: 6:00pm–10:00pm
Friday and Saturday: 6:00pm–11:00pm
Sunday: 5:30pm–10:00pm
Lunch:
Monday–Friday: 12:00pm–3:00pm

Hoo–boy! (Expensive)

VF 🍸

NUTRISSERIE DELI

142 West 72nd Street
(Near Broadway)
(212) 799–2454

Once a pleasant natural–foods "lunch counter" (dinner too) in the rear of a well–stocked health food store, Nutrisserie has expanded. They now can boast genuine tables and a totally vegan–friendly bill of fare that uses no salt, sugar, dairy, and only organically raised produce They have a very nice menu, which includes such tasty tidbits as Vegetable Roti, BBQ T.V.P. Ribs, Tofu Spinach Rolls, and much, much more. Their 3-Salad Combo Plate allows you to choose from around 26 items and design your own dish. They also make Health Shakes, such as the Stress Shake, which includes Brewer's Yeast, Fiber, Organic Bananas, Soy Milk, and Vitari. If you're a fan of Wheatgrass Juice, theirs at $1.25 a hit is a bargain. Incidentally, and apropos of nothing, Tiny Tim shops here. Tiptoe through the tulips...

Monday–Saturday: 11:00am–8:30pm
Sunday: 11:00am–7:30pm

Moderate

Ve   **O**   &

RYOTA'S TING

(718) 217-0583

Wonderful, totally vegan, African-American food service providing catering and home delivery as well as selling at street fairs. Our favorite dish is the Bar-B-Q Gluten "Ribs," but they have a couple of dozen other greats as well. Some standouts are the Tofu Orange "Duck," and the Soy "Sausage" Pepper and Onion (a veggie version of those insidious meat things so common at street fairs).

Days: Whenever & wherever they pop up
(call for a schedule) or

Call for home delivery or catering.

Inexpensive

Ve   ♿

OASIS

137 Seventh Avenue
(Near Carroll Street)
Park Slope, Brooklyn
(718) 783–0215

Middle Eastern cuisine. Our ilk may dine here with impunity since they serve Falafel, Humous, Baba Ghanoush, Omelets, and Salads. If you don't do dairy, you have to make a point of telling them or they'll assume otherwise (we ordered grape leaves, which automatically came covered with yogurt). We found the servings to be a bit skimpy and the prices a bit high. If you're looking for high–quality food at a reasonable price, this place is less an oasis than a mirage.

Sunday–Thursday: 11:00am–10:30pm
Friday & Saturday: 11:00am–11:30pm

Moderate

VF   ♿

OXU

566 Amsterdam Avenue
(Near 87th Street)
(212) 787–8316

Austere, macrobiotic, Japanese restaurant on the Upper West Side with a somewhat regular crowd and a very high-quality menu. Some of the goodies we enjoyed were the Mabo Tofu (Stir–fried Tofu with ground Seitan, Broccoli, and Fungi in a Black Bean Sauce) and the Ozu Croquette (Couscous, Millet, Kasha, and Lentils), which comes with a choice of Tofu, Seitan, or Beet Sauce and which is served with a Green Salad. Our daughter enjoyed the Soba Mariko, which is noodles sautéed with Vegetables in Tomato–Miso sauce and served with a deep–fried Seitan Cutlet. She claimed that "It almost tasted like spaghetti." If you suffer from "Tofu–phobia" (an all–too–common disease afflicting millions) please come here. They serve 50,000 kinds of Tofu prepared 60,000 different ways. Well, perhaps we're stretching the truth just a bit. However, the selection is quite broad. Desserts are well prepared and include many non–dairy, sugar–free yummies such as the Almond Creme Caramel. Like many macrobiotic restaurants, they also serve fish.

Sunday–Thursday: 12:00pm–10:00pm
Friday and Saturday: 12:00pm–10:00pm

Moderate–Expensive

Ve

PITA CUISINE

535 LaGuardia Place (212) 254–1417
65 Spring Street (212) 966–2529

Cafeteria–style restaurants serving salads and hot, meatless entrees as well as lots of things in Pita. Some items for us include: Vegetarian Chili (which we found sort of bland), Veggie Nuggets, Meatless Moussaka (which was pretty good), and more. Good hang–out joints. They also serve some meat things for you butt–biters out there (pork butt, that is).

LaGuardia Place:
Monday–Friday: 11:00am–9:00pm
Saturday and Sunday: 12:00pm–9:00pm

Spring Street:
Monday–Friday: 8:30am–8:00pm
Saturday and Sunday: 12:00pm–6:00pm

Inexpensive

VF

PIZZARINI NATUREL

2812 Ocean Avenue
(Near Avenue X)
Sheepshead Bay, Brooklyn
(718) 648–4248

"Health–food" style restaurant with Whole Wheat Vegetable Pizza and a large selection of Salads. Nice atmosphere. Maple–sweetened, Whole–Wheat Apple Pie is available for dessert. While they're not totally vegetarian, they do serve quite a few things for lacto and lacto–ovo type folks. Not a heckuva lot for vegans, though.

Monday–Friday: 11:00am–10:00pm
Saturday & Sunday: 12:00pm–11:00pm

Moderate

VF   ♿

PLANET ONE

76 East 7th Street
(Near 1st Avenue)
(212) 475–0112

The atmosphere at Planet One is warm and friendly, and the prices are inexpensive. When we last ate there, the soup of the day, a Red Lentil with Squash, was delicious, and reminded us of a thick curried dahl. The Roti, a Whole Wheat Jamaican Bread filled with Curried Vegetable Stew, Red Cabbage, Zucchini, and Carrots, was super. The going price for Roti on Church Avenue is half as much, but one has to consider the trendy East Village rent. The Vegetable Plate is a good deal as well. We had the Collard Greens, West African Rice, and African Okra. A companion who usually hates Okra loved this. It's cooked with Garlic, Tomatoes, and Spinach. The owners, Maima and Annette, are very nice, and are only too happy to cater to most folks' diets. Primarily vegetarian, but some seafood and free–range chicken is served.

Seven days: 12:00pm–12:00am
Inexpensive

VF ♿

PLUM TREE

1501 First Avenue
(Between 78th & 79th Streets)
(212) 734–1412

Macrobiotic cuisine with an emphasis on the food of Asia. Try the Soy Corn Bread or Woman Warrior Stew (Tofu, Seitan, Veggies, and Burdock). Brunch is also available from 12:00pm–4:00pm on Saturdays and Sundays—with such wonderful choices as Buckwheat Pancakes or Scrambled Tofu.

Tuesday–Sunday: 12:00pm–10:00pm
Mondays: Closed

Moderate

Ve   ☯   ♿

QUANTUM LEAP

88 West 3rd Street
(Between Thompson & Sullivan)
(212) 677–8050

Longtime mainstay for vegetarians in New York. This is the direct descendent of the original Quantum Leap in Queens, which, by the way, is still alive and kicking. Try the daily special Casseroles, Salads, Soups, and Tempura, as well as the weekend brunch including Whole Grain Pancakes and Waffles. Scott Bakula eats here (a little show–biz humor).

Monday–Thursday: 11:00am–10:45pm
Friday and Saturday: 11:00am–11:45pm
Sunday: 11:00am–10:00pm

Moderate

V &

QUANTUM LEAP

65–64 Fresh Meadow Lane
Fresh Meadows, Queens
(718) 461–1307

The precursor to the branch in the Village. One of the oldest continuous Veggie restaurants in N.Y. They have Casseroles, Salads, Soups, and Tempura, as well as a weekend brunch including Whole Grain Pancakes and Waffles. Try the daily specials. The Mexican Fiesta is good, and so is the Seitan Parmigiana. The Miso Soup has lots of vegetables in it. Sample the Sweet Potato Tempura as well. Good Tofu Desserts. Well-stocked natural-foods store next door. Pleasant atmosphere in a neighborhood that, for New York, is positively bucolic. The last few times we were there, though, we felt that the quality of the food had been slipping.

Tuesday–Thursday: 11:00am–10:30pm
Friday and Saturday: 11:00am–11:00pm
Sunday: 10:00am–9:30pm
Mondays: Closed

Moderate

V   ♿

RATHER'S DAIRY RESTAURANT

138 Delancey Street
(Between Norfolk & Suffolk Streets)
(212) 677–5588

Oy, such food! Kosher dairy restaurant supreme.
The three "B"s: Blintzes, Bagels, and Borscht (and
that's just for appetizers). Lots of kosher fish
dishes too (so the fish find religion before they're
slaughtered–that's nice). Wise guy waiters. Bring
lots of dough. Hey, maybe afterwards you could
go shopping on Orchard Street and find a bargain.
Actually, the days of bargains on Orchard Street
are long gone.

Sunday–Thursday: 6:00am–10:30pm
Friday: 6:00am–3:00pm
Saturday: Closed

Expensive

V   ♿

RED HOT SZECHUAN

347 7th Avenue (10th Street)
Park Slope, Brooklyn
(718) 369–0700; 0702

Vegetarian Chinese food has come to Brooklyn,
and the quality is pretty high. The Sauteed Veggie

"Pork" with Bar-B-Q Sauce is scrumptious—served with Snow Peas, Onions and a "fish" carved out of a Zucchini as a garnish. The Sweet and Sour "Ribs" are great and the Hot and Sour Soup is excellent.

Monday–Thursday: 11:00am–10:30pm
Friday & Saturday: 11:30am–11:00pm
Sunday: 12:30pm–10:30pm

Moderate–Expensive

v   &

SALAD BOWL
906 Third Ave. (Near 55th Street) (212) 644–6767
Pier 17, South Street Seaport (212) 693–0590
901 6th Avenue (A&S Plaza) (212) 594–6512
566 7th Avenue (Near 41st Street)
(212) 921–7060

All–natural–food restaurants featuring on–premises cooking and baking. Quite a lot for vegetarians–to wit: Vegetable Cheese Casserole, Vegetable Lasagna, Vegetarian Chili, Eggplant Parmigiana, Veggie Burgers, and of course lots and lots of salads. The list is long, and a lot of the food is Vegetarian or Vegan. Don't miss their scrumptious desserts either, all baked on the premises. We're partial to the Cranberry Bread ourselves.

Seven days: 7:00am–9:00pm
(Varies according to site—call first)

Inexpensive

VF   ♿

SALAD DAZE

690 Third Avenue
(Between 43 & 44th Streets)
(212) 953–DAYS

Cafeteria–style (you line up and order, then bring it to your table) salad joint with a high-quality selection that includes a goodly number of meatless salads as well. One of our favorites is the Salad Daze Specialty (Romaine Lettuce, Plum Tomatoes, Red Peppers, Mushrooms, Cucumbers, Red Onions, and Avocado Pesto). They also have a large number of delicious Pasta dishes. Quality is always high, and prices are quite reasonable.
Monday–Friday: 7:30am–6:00pm
Saturday and Sunday: Closed

Inexpensive

VF

SANCTUARY

33 Saint Marks Place (8th Street)
(between 2nd & 3rd Avenues)
(212) 505–8234

The Sanctuary is primarily an interfaith spiritual center offering symposia and lectures on a wide variety of religious topics. However, if your aim is nothing more than a gratifying discourse between your stomach, tongue, and wallet, they have a vegetarian buffet that is both good and cheap. Check this out: $5.00—we said $5.00—for all you can eat! (Come hungry and make them prove it.) The offerings are mostly Vegan and primarily Indian or Middle–Eastern. Check out the Vegetarian Chili (T.V.P. and Tofu) if they have it.

Tuesday–Saturday: 12:00pm–8:30pm
Sunday & Monday: Closed

Inexpensive

V   ♿

SAN LOCO

129 Second Avenue
(Near Saint Marks Place)
(212) 260–7948

Funky Mexican take–out type joint in the swingin' East Village, man. A good number of vegetarian items are available, since the beans are made without lard or beefal matter. In fact, they have a small section on their menu just for us. They do have seats and tables, but it still feels like a take–out joint. If that sounds cryptic, go and you'll know what I mean. Best time to visit is 3:00am for the optimal hallucinatory effect.

Sunday–Thursday: 11:00am–4:00am
Friday and Saturday: 10:30am–5:00am
Inexpensive

VF   ♿

SAVE THE CHILDREN VEGETARIAN RESTAURANT

797 Washington Avenue
(Entrance on Lincoln Place)
Crown Heights, Brooklyn
(718) 622-9731

West Indian, Rastafarian, totally vegan restaurant. The food is really good and really inexpensive. They're one block from the Brooklyn Museum and two blocks from the Brooklyn Botanical Gardens. For $7.00, we got a platter with a little bit of everything. Included were Vegetarian Duck (Tofu Skin), which was fantastic, Okra with Soya Granules—delish, Rice and Peas, Salad, and Plantains. One entree with Rice and Peas will cost you $5.00. They serve Vegetarian Rotis, which tend to go fast, and they've recently installed a steam table, which will soon be in operation offering hot vegan goodies. They sell a good selection of natural groceries as well.

Monday–Saturday: 11:00am–10:00pm
Sunday: Closed
Inexpensive
Ve   &

SCALLIONS

48 Trinity Place
(Near Rector Street)
(212) 480–9135

This location used to be the home of the legendary "Country Life" (a Seventh-Day-Adventist-owned banquet-style strictly-vegan restaurant). Scallions is similar to its predecessor in many regards. They provide a superlative Vegan buffet that's paid for by the pound and they have specials changing daily. They also have a "deli" counter which features such things as Vegetarian Burgers and assorted Sandwiches. Definitely worth the visit.

Monday–Friday: 7:30am–6:00pm
Saturday and Sunday: Closed
Moderate
Ve

SHEM TOV DAIRY RESTAURANT

1040 46th Street
(Near 10th Avenue)
Borough Park, Brooklyn
(718) 438–9366

In previous editions of our guide, we gave Shem Tov (which ironically translates as "The Good Name") an abysmal review, prattling on about the "low quality of the food" and "the flies getting the best of everything." Well, we ate there again recently, and guess what? It's not so bad anymore. In fact, some of the food is almost good. So, if you're in Borough Park or visiting someone at Maimonides Hospital (and Taam Eden is closed) give Shem Tov a visit. They still may have a lot of flies in the summer, though.

Sunday–Thursday: 8:00am–8:00pm
Friday and Saturday: Closed
Still not as cheap as you would expect.

V   &

SMILE OF THE BEYOND

86–14 Parsons Boulevard
(Near Hillside Avenue)
Jamaica, Queens
(718) 739–7453

Vegetarian luncheonette that serves breakfast and lunch and that is affiliated with Sri Chinmoy and the Annam Brahma restaurant nearby. The place has a beautiful sky blue decor and an old–fashioned soda machine with vintage 70's logos. The waiters are disciples of Sri Chinmoy, and the quality of the food is pretty high. Try the "Turkey" Club Sandwich, the Soy "Steak" Burger, or the Vegetarian "B.L.T."—all meatless. The Chocolate Cake with Vanilla Icing was quite sweet.

Monday–Friday: 7:00am–4:00pm
Saturday: 7:00am–3:00pm
Sunday: Closed
Inexpensive
V

SOUEN

28 East 13th Street
(Between University Place & 5th Avenue)
(212) 627–7150

210 6th Avenue
(Near Prince Street)
(212) 807–7421

Macrobiotic restaurant supreme. If you can't find it here, you're in bad shape, pal. No meat, eggs, or dairy, although they do serve fish, and they try to get organic produce when they can. Try the Seitan Cutlets, Tempeh Croquettes, Noodles with Kuzu Sauce (Carrot & Burdock), or just have a bowl of the best Miso Soup in New York. Have you ever had Seitan Sushi? Good stuff for breakfast too—like Mochi Waffles, even. For some inexplicable reason, the branch on 13th street is much better than the one in Soho. "Souen" means "green garden" in Japanese.

Monday–Friday: 10:00–10:00pm
Saturday and Sunday: 10:00am–11:00pm

Moderate

Ve   ♿

SPRING STREET NATURAL

62 Spring Street
(Entrance on Lafayette Street)
(212) 966–0290

Wonderful, atmospheric restaurant in Soho providing elegantly prepared dishes with a preponderance of organically raised ingredients. Although they serve fish, chicken and dairy, they have quite a good selection for vegetarians and vegans. Try the Tempeh Burger or the Semolina Fettucini with Shiitake Mushrooms. The Corn-fried Seitan with Dipping Sauce is delicious as well.

Sunday–Thursday: 11:30am–12:00am
Friday and Saturday: 11:30am–1:00am

Moderate

VF

STEVE & SONS BAKERY, RESTAURANT & CATERERS

9305 Church Avenue
(Near East 93rd Street)
Brownsville, Brooklyn
(718) 498–6800

West Indian (Grenadian) restaurant–bakery in Brownsville. Steve and Sons prepares many vegetarian dishes using Wheat Gluten. A particular favorite of ours is the Vegetarian B.B.Q. "Ribs." All the entrees are served with Rice and Peas. This is the "Home of the Vegetarian Patties"—their meatless version of the West Indian staple. It's made with Soy Protein and a Whole Wheat crust (if you specifically ask for Whole Wheat). Their freshly made desserts are fantastic, and we never go home without a loaf of "Hot-From-The-Oven" Whole Wheat Bread.

Monday–Thursday: 7:00am–12:00am
Friday: 7:00am–6:00pm
Saturday: 6:00pm–12:00am
Sunday: 7:30am–12:00pm

Inexpensive

VF ♿

STRICTLY ROOTS

2058 Adam Clayton Powell Blvd.
(Between 122nd & 123rd Streets)
(212) 864–8699

A sign on the wall states: Strictly Roots "serves nothing that crawls, walks, swims or flies". Totally vegan Rastafarian restaurant and take–out. You ask for the platter size you want: small for $4.50, medium for $7.00, large for $9.00 and then choose the foods to go in it. The Rice and Peas and the Veggie Duck were both delicious. Nice decor too.

Seven days: 9:00am–10:30pm
Inexpensive

Ve ♿

TAAM-EDER KOSHER DAIRY RESTAURANT

5001 13th Avenue
(Near 50th Street)
Boro Park, Brooklyn
(718) 972–1692

Kosher Dairy restaurant in the heart of Boro Park. Blintzes, Latkes, Stuffed Cabbage (the veggie style), Vegetarian "Liver," Kugels, the usual culprits, but all prepared very, very well. As a matter of fact, the quality here is exceptional. Take-out is available, and you have the choice of dining in either their informal coffee–shop type are in the front, or the Catskills–style dining room in the rear.

Sunday–Thursday: 9:00am–9:00pm
Friday: 9:00am–2:00pm
Saturday: Closed

Moderate in the front
Expensive in the back

v

TAMARIND SEED

2935 Broadway
(Near 115th Street)
(212) 864–3360

Seventy–five percent Natural Foods store, twenty–five percent Salad Bar, Sandwiches, and Steam Table. Some choices here include: Chili over Rice, Tempeh Sandwiches, and more. You can have a seat upstairs if you like and get ready for that big test you're gonna cheat on at Columbia or Barnard.

Monday–Friday: 8:00am–10:00pm
Saturday: 9:00am–10:00pm

Sunday: 9:00am–9:00pm

Inexpensive

VF

TAQUERIA

72 7th Avenue
(Between Berkeley & Lincoln Place)
Park Slope, Brooklyn
(718) 398–4300

341 7th Avenue
(Between 9th & 10th Streets)
Park Slope, Brooklyn
(718) 624–7498

8 Bergen St. (Near Court Street)
Cobble Hill, Brooklyn
(718) 624–7498

355 Sixth Avenue
(Near Waverly Place)
Manhattan
(212) 229–0999

"Authentic" East L.A. Mexican Food—very good, hearty "stick–to–your–ribs" fare. The Vegetarian Burrito at $6.25 is a meal for the day. Quality is quite high. Try the Vegetarian Taco or the San Juaquin Burrito (all vegetarian), or just get some Rice and Beans. Although they do use a lot of Sour Cream and Cheese in many of the dishes, you can request that your food be prepared without dairy and they'll gladly comply. Who knows— perhaps the day will come when we'll see a Taqueria on every street corner in America.

Seven days: 12:00pm–11:00pm
(Some variance according to location)
Moderate

VF   &

TEMPLE IN THE VILLAGE

74 West 3rd Street
(Between LaGuardia Place & Thompson Street)
(212) 475–5670

Small, buffet–style natural–food restaurant with good Veggies, Noodles, and Grains. In other words, an extensive natural, vegetarian salad bar. Help yourself, brother. Reminds us a little of a soup kitchen. Hallelujah! If the weather's nice, get yourself a heapin' helpin', go to Washington Square Park, and listen to some Bob Dylan wannabe.

Monday–Saturday: 11:00am–10:00pm
Sunday: Closed
Inexpensive
V

TEVA NATURAL FOODS

122 East 42nd Street
(Near Lexington Avenue)
(Chanin Bldg.–downstairs)

(212) 599–1265

Kosher Dairy Middle–Eastern joint serving Falafel, Baba Ghanoush, Vegetarian Chopped Liver, Vegetable Cutlets, and more. They're in the concourse level of the Chanin building (downstairs) on your way to the subway. Nice people, good food. Right near Grand Central Station.

Monday–Friday: 7:00am–5:00pm
Saturday and Sunday: Closed
Inexpensive

V   ✡

TOPAZ

127 West 56th Street
(Between 6th & 7th Avenues)
(212) 957–8020

High-quality Thai restaurant with a good number of vegetarian entrees, many of which are vegan and all of which are quite beautifully prepared (some with rose petals). Some recommended choices are the Vegetarian Duck, the Vegetables and Pepper in Coconut Milk Curry, and the Gang Som Pak Soup (which is made with Corn, Cabbage, and Thai Herbs—it smells terrible, but tastes delicious).

Monday–Thursday: 11:00am–11:00pm
Friday: 11:00am–4:30pm
Saturday: 4:00pm–11:30pm
Sunday: 4:00pm–11:00pm

Moderate–Expensive

VF

TWO BOOTS

37 Ave A (Between 2nd & 3rd Streets)
Lower East Side
(212) 505–2276

514 2nd Street (Near Seventh Avenue)
Park Slope, Brooklyn
(718) 499–3253

The two boots in the title symbolize the geographical boots of Italy and Louisiana. Consequently Two Boots' cuisine is a combination of Italian and Cajun. The food is superb, the atmosphere is splendid, and they welcome children (although the Park Slope branch is far more child friendly). They have quite a few Veggie items on the menu. Have a Thin Crust Pizza topped with almost any assortment of Veggies. Some say this is the best Pizza in N.Y. Quite an accomplishment.

Tuesday–Sunday: 11:00am–11:00pm
Mondays: Closed

Moderate

VF

UDUPI PALACE

35–66 73rd Street
(Near Roosevelt Avenue)
Jackson Heights, Queens
(718) 507–1600

Good, cheap Vegetarian Indian vittles in Jacky
Heights (also known as "Little India"). Most
dishes are under $6.00, except for the Curries,
which are mostly $6.25, and full dinners (6 courses
and up), which range from $11.00 to $13.00. The
lunch special is a particularly good deal. Some
goodies: Medhu Vada (Fried Lentil Donuts) are
simply scrumptious. Dip them in Sambar and a
delicious Chutney made with Coconut and
Cilantro. The Gobi Masala Curry (Cauliflower and
spices), the Kancheepurum Iddly (Lentil Patties
with Cashews, Ginger, and Coriander), and the
Coconut Uthappam are all superb as well. If you
frequent South Indian restaurants, you know that
Thali means a platter with Rice and Papadam
(crispy bread) in the middle and various small
dishes surrounding it. This is a nice combination
of various tastes, from the very hot Rasam, a traditional South Indian-style soup, to cool Raita, a
traditional Yogurt-based condiment designed to
cool off your tongue. The Masala Dosai was very
impressive—huge Crepes filled with Potatoes,
Onions, Carrots, and Nuts. The Badam Halwa
(Ground Almonds cooked in Honey & Butter) for
dessert was simply wonderful.

Seven days: 12:00pm–9:45pm

Moderate

V   &

UPTOWN JUICE BAR
(AND VEGETARIAN DELI)

60 West 125th Street
(Between 5th and Lenox Avenues)
(212) 987–1188

Veggie sandwiches (Ital "Chicken," "Beef," and "Turkey"), Veggie Burgers, Salads, and of course a vast selection of juices.

Monday–Saturday: 9:00am–8:00pm
Sunday: Closed

Inexpensive

Ve   &

VEGA HOUSE

66 West 45th Street
(Between 5th & 6th Avenues)
(212) 354-5849

Brand new vegetarian Asian restaurant with a huge vegan menu including such goodies as: Sutra Bundles (Zucchini, Asparagus, Basil, Black Mushroom, and Water Chestnuts wrapped with Soy Protein) and Curry Vege "Chicken" (Chunks of Soy Protein stewed with Potatoes, Carrots, and Celery in a Curry Sauce). Lots more. News flash: As of press time, they've done a 360 and become a fairly standard, run of the mill, Chinese restaurant. We decided to include them anyway in the hope that many of our readers will go in, ask to see Jimmy (the owner), and urge them to return to a vegetarian menu.

Monday-Friday: 11:00am-10:00pm
Saturday: 12:00pm-10:00pm
Sunday: 12:00pm-9:00pm

Moderate

V &

VEGETABLE GARDEN

15 East 40th Street
(Between 5th & Madison Avenues)
(212) 545-7444

Formerly an outpost of "The Great American Health Bar," this place is swell. They sport a large, very clean dining area which is divided nicely into separate rooms for smoking and nonsmoking and they also have a spiffy-looking counter up front if you're really rushed. Now to the food. The Salads are fresh and healthy. They have a bunch of Soups that you can get with extras like Brown Rice, a Muffin, or a Salad as well as a bevy of Baked Potatoes, which are available stuffed with the likes of Vegetarian Chili or Steamed Vegetables. While there is an emphasis on Fish and Dairy (it being a kosher dairy restaurant and all), lots of other goodies are available as well. The Hot Vegetable Cutlet Sandwich was pretty durn good and they had no problem whatsoever with "holding" the cheese that normally tops it. It was served quickly and elegantly with a salad and a side of French Fries. They also have some nice entrees like Vegetable Lasagna, Oriental Vegetables over Brown Rice, and specials which change daily. Breakfasts are pretty standard fare (eggs and fries), with a few notable exceptions—you can get a Bowl of Granola or some piping hot Oatmeal served with honey, as well as a variety of freshly squeezed juices.

Monday–Thursday: 7:00am–7:00pm
Friday: 7:00am–3:00pm
Saturday and Sunday: Closed
Inexpensive
V

VEGE VEGE JJ

544 Third Avenue
(Between 36th & 37th Streets)
(212) 679–4710/4702

Wonderful, extremely-elegant, totally-vegetarian, certified-kosher, positively-scrumptious Asian restaurant. The chef and co-owner here, Mama Pang, was formerly the chef at Zen Palate, and the quality of the food, both in taste and presentation, reflects the standard of that restaurant without being nearly as snooty. In fact, all of the staff are quite gracious and extremely solicitous of their customers' comfort. For appetizers, try the Moo Shu Basil Rolls (marvelous, filled with nuts and wrapped in basil) or sample the Barbe-cued, Grilled Satay (made from Gluten). As for the main course, the selection is so broad that you may find it difficult to decide. The Curried Veg-etarian "Chicken" is quite good and almost indis-tinguishable from a hearty stew, and the "Chicken"–A la King is superb. We recently had a Veggie "Lamb" there that was unbelievable, and made totally out of mushrooms. The artistry in the presentation of the dishes is truly amazing, and they have a fully stocked bar as well. This is an excellent place to bring potential "converts."

Seven days: 11:30am–11:00pm

Moderate

Ve

VEGETARIAN DELIGHTS (AND MEAT DISHES)

3604 Clarendon Road
(Near East 36th Street)
Flatbush, Brooklyn
(718) 284–9605

Take–out joint serving Rastafarian-style vegetar-ian dishes and West Indian meat dishes as well. Some specialties include Jamaican Veggie Patties and more! We had Vegetable Roti–like a stew wrapped up in a Pancake (pretty good), Tofu Din-ner (Spicy Fried Tofu with Veggies) a dish called Ital Stew (Various Vegetables, Rice and Peas, Salad, and whatnot–watch out for twigs). (We think the chef had a little too much ganja, mon.) Ackee and Vegetables is a nice combination. (Ackee is a West-Indian nut-like fruit.) Desserts include Sweet Potato Pudding, Corn Meal Pudding, and Carrot Cake. Breakfast is available as well.

Monday–Saturday: 9:00am–12:00am
Sunday: Closed

Inexpensive

VF

VEGETARIAN HEAVEN

304 West 58th Street
(4 Columbus Circle)
Near 8th Avenue
(212) 956–4678

Pretty good vegetarian Chinese restaurant with a huge menu. Sister restaurant of Bamboo Garden in Flushing. It's a short walk to the Theater District for you tourist types. Try one of the many varieties of "Chicken" or "Beef" or the Barbecued "Ribs." The best bet is the lunch specials—a heapin' helpin' of vittles for only $3.95. The only problem this place seems to have is that the service is often very, very slow. Incidentally, this joint is certified kosher by the one of the great Jewish holymen of our age.

Seven days: 11:00am–11:30pm

Moderate–Expensive

V

VEGETARIAN'S PARADISE III

33–35 Mott Street
(212) 406–6988/2896.

VP returns to Chinatown! Millions cheer! Lucky Lindy is carried off by scores of cheering Frenchmen—oops, wrong article... Many of you may know of VP only through VP2 or VP2–GO in the Village. However, the original Vegetarian Paradise (VP–1 for those with a calculator) was the first Vegetarian restaurant in New York. It was located on the Bowery near Canal in Chinatown, and closed a year and a half ago due to structural damage in the building. VPIII boasts a clean, roomy, well-designed space that is also wheelchair-accessible, as well as the yummy grub that made them famous.

Sunday–Thursday: 11:00am–10:00pm
Friday & Saturday: 11:00am–11:00pm

Moderate

Ve   &

VILLAGE NATURAL

46 Greenwich Avenue
(Between 6th & 7th Avenues)
(212) 727–0968

Excellent, moderately priced vegetarian restaurant in the West Village. We enjoyed the Seitan Parmigiana (excellent), Soba (Buckwheat Noodles) with Tahini (super), and a Tostada Platter with everything (beans, cheese, guacamole, sour cream), which was filling and satisfying. Good Fruit Tofu Pies too—sweetened with maple syrup.

Monday–Thursday: 11:00am–11:00pm
Friday: 11:00am–12:00am
Saturday, Sunday: 11:00am–10:00pm

Moderate

V   &

VP 2

144 West 4th Street
(Near 6th Avenue)
(212) 260–7130

VP 2 GO

140 West 4th Street
(Also Near 6th Avenue)

Progeny of the justly famous Vegetarian's Paradise in Chinatown. VP 2 is simply a more elegant, expensive version of the original downtown location (which just happens to have been the first vegetarian Chinese restaurant in N.Y.) The portions here are a little smaller than the original, too. VP 2 GO, as one might expect, is for take–out, and offers an excellent selection of macrobiotic dim sum. You'll have a very good, elegant dining experience here, and the Village location is great, but try VP-III on Mott street for the best value.

Sunday–Tuesday and Thursday: 11:30am–9:30pm
Wednesday: Closed
Friday and Saturday: 11:30am–10:30pm

Expensive

Ve

WEISS' KOSHER DAIRY RESTAURANT

1146 Coney Island Avenue
(Near Avenue H)
Midwood, Brooklyn
(718) 421–0184

Pursuant to kosher edicts, dairy restaurants permit absolutely no meat or meat products on the premises (if you don't count fish). Some specialties here include: Blintzes (Cheese, Potato, Blueberry), Kasha Varnishkas (Buckwheat Groats with Bowtie Noodles), Vegetable "Steak" with Mushroom Sauce, and a pretty good Vegetarian Shepherd's Pie. All you can eat Monday nights. Quality is high. Atmosphere is Catskills to the gills. They have a $10 per plate minimum no matter what you eat, so beware!

Sunday–Thursday: 12:00pm–10:00pm
Friday: 12:00pm-a few hours before sundown
Closed Saturday until 90 minutes after sundown

Expensive

V   🦽

WEST INDIAN VEGETARIAN AND SEAFOOD RESTAURANT

752 Nostrand Avenue
(Between Park & Sterling)
Crown Heights, Brooklyn
(718) 778-1700

Dinky little take–out joint frequently permeated with the smell of fresh herb. The Chiclet Stew is made from a Worthington product (which we believe has MSG) yet still tastes good. The Macaroni & Cheese was great, as was the Stir Fried Cabbage and of course the Rice and Peas.

Seven days: 8:00am–8:30pm

Inexpensive

VF

WHOLE EARTH BAKERY AND KITCHEN

70 Spring Street
(Between Broadway & Lafayette Streets)
Soho
(212) 226-8280

130 St. Marks (Near Avenue A)
East Village
(212) 677-7597

Bakery and Kitchen—whole-earthwise, that is. This concludes our Newspeak lesson for today, Winston. How much is 2 + 2? But seriously folks, they make delicious natural baked goods, such as Cakes, Cookies, and Muffins, most of which contain no sugar, honey, or dairy products and are strictly vegan. They also have assorted extras like Raisin Bun Sandwiches, Cheese Biscuits, Whole–Wheat Poppyseed Crackers, Tofu Veggie Rolls, Cabbage or Black Bean Turnovers, Made–to–Order Cakes, and Juices galore. Their motto is: "simple food for complex times." 'Nuf said.

Monday–Saturday: 8:00am–9:00pm
Sunday: 10:00am–8:00pm

Moderate

v

WHOLE FOODS IN SOHO

117 Prince Street
(Between Greene & Wooster Streets)
(212) 673–5388

Natural market/deli with a huge and wonderful salad bar. Not a restaurant, but definitely worth knowing about if you're in the area and need a little nosh to tide you over. They have an incredible steam table with plenty of things for our ilk, and a fairly well–stocked natural–foods store to boot. Strictly take–out.

Seven days: 9:00am–9:30pm

Moderate

V

WHOLE WHEAT 'N WILD BERRIES

57 West 10th Street
(Near Sixth Avenue)
(212) 677–3410

Delicious vegetarian cuisine in a "homespun" setting. Whole Wheat 'n Wild Berries is a longtime mainstay of New York's vegetarian community, having been around since 1971. Try the Nutburger (Walnuts, Cashews, Rice, Onions, Eggs, and Spices on an English Muffin) or the Small Planet Casserole (Steamed Veggies, Rice, and Nuts in Mushroom Sauce). Cheese seems to be in almost everything, but they're pretty accommodating and will leave it off if you stand up on your chair and demand it. Don't miss the Chocolate Marble Tofu Pudding. It's outrageous. They also serve fish. (Mommy, they killed Flipper!)

Monday–Sunday dinner: 5:00pm–11:00pm
Tuesday–Saturday lunch: 11:30am–4:30pm
Sunday brunch: 11:30am–4:30pm

Moderate–Expensive

V   &

WHO'S ON SEVENTH?

183 Seventh Avenue
(Near First Street)
Park Slope, Brooklyn
(718) 965–0597

"Natural"–style restaurant, which claims to make
everything from scratch. Weekend brunches are
served with Fresh Fruit, and include Whole Grain
Pancakes or Vegetable Omelets. The Yellow Corn
Enchilada is o.k. The Tofu Sunflower Burger is
so–so. Non-dairy dishes are available as well.
Park-Slope–style prices. Bottom line, though: the
management is blasé and the overall quality is
bland, bland, bland.

Seven days: 11:00am–11:00pm
Saturday and Sunday brunch: 11:00am–4:00pm

Moderate–expensive

v   &

WOK NATURALLY

37 East 29th Street
(Between Park and Madison Avenues)
(212) 685–1438/1481

Totally vegan Chinese restaurant with a gigantic
selection. They offer over 170 different entrees
and 32 lunch specials. The lunch specials are particularly great deals at $3.95 each. This restau-
rant, like Hong Kong Vegetarian uptown, is an
offshoot of the renowned House of Vegetarian on

Mott Street in Chinatown.

Monday–Saturday: 11:00am–10:30pm
Sunday: 12:00pm–10:30pm

Moderate

Ve   ♿

YONAH SHJMMEL'S

137 East Houston Street
(Between 1st & 2nd Avenues)
(212) 477–2858

You haven't had a knish until you've been here.
All kinds knishes and handmade too. Kasha,
Cheese, Potato, ad infinitum. It's not kosher, but
it's been here about a hundred years or so, and
there's good reason. Try the 100-year-old Yogurt—don't worry, it was in the fridge—we mean
the culture for the Yogurt is 100 years old—oh,
you know what we mean.

Seven days: 8:00am–7:00pm
Inexpensive

v   ✡   ♿

ZEN PALATE

633 9th Avenue
(Entrance on 46th Street)
(212) 582–1669

34 Union Square East
(Near 16th Street)
(212) 614–9345

Vegetarian Oriental "bistro" on restaurant row (W. 46th Street). Snooty and expensive, but the food is good. (They had a great guiding force at their inception–see Vege Vege II). The Hot and Sour Vegetable Soup is excellent, as are the Vegetable Dumplings. For an entree, the "Sweet and Sour Divine" (Deep fried pecan puffs with sweet and sour peppers) was delish. For dessert we had the "Sweet Black Sesame Pastry," which were four surprisingly tiny cookies with Sesame Paste filling. Recently opened: Zen Palate(II) in the yup–and–coming Union Square vicinity—downstairs: cheap and friendly, upstairs: expensive and snooty. Gee, we're sorry, we're supposed to pay you all that money and take crap from the waiters? We don't think so! Not so incidently: in an article in *New York* magazine dated 5/30/94, Zen Palate's Tofu Cheesecake was revealed to be laced with real Cream Cheese (and to have 399 calories and 24.5 gms. of fat per slice).

Monday–Friday: 11:30pm–10:45pm
Saturday: 11:00am-11:00pm
Sunday: 12:00pm–10:30pm

Expensive

V

ZUCCHINI

1336 1st Avenue
(Between 71st & 72nd Streets)
(212) 249–0559

This is the type of food that scares people away from a vegetarian diet. The meatless items that we had were bland and boring. Our dining companions both ordered chicken dishes and thought they were great. We therefore conclude that the chefs here must feel that people who don't want meat also don't want flavor. The good news is that the atmosphere is very nice, and although we found the food quite bland, there are plenty of meatless items to choose from. The service is sl–o–o–ow. They have an early–bird special from 4:00 to 7:00 (entree, coffee or tea, and dessert) for $9.95. A 10% discount is available to patrons of Sotheby's and Christie's. Plenty o' snob appeal.

Seven days: 11:00am–10:30pm

Expensive

who is so mean to eat them? You?

A GLOSSARY OF TERMS FOR THE BEGINNER

Broiled: A method of cooking in which a food is heated by radiant heat rather than by conduction. In other words, the heat is transferred directly from the source rather than by the metal of a pan.

Gluten: A protein complex which, when water is added to it, becomes elastic and has a characteristic texture. Formation of gluten enhances the rising of bread with the help of leavening. Seitan is made from wheat gluten.

Macrobiotic: The application of specific ancient oriental philosophies to diet. The concepts of yin and yang are applied to the alkaline and acid qualities in foods, with the goal of having a neutral Ph diet. Local foods are encouraged, and are often Japanese or Japanese-style cuisine.

Miso: A fermented soybean paste. It's made from soybeans, starter, salt, and occasionally rice or barley. It can be diluted and eaten as a soup or added undiluted to many foods as a seasoning.

Rennet: Used in the curdling of milk for cheese making. Obtained from the stomach lining of calves, lambs, kids, or pigs. Some cheeses use vegetable rennet.

Seitan: Wheat gluten separated from the other components of wheat and cooked in soy sauce. It has a characteristic flavor and texture somewhat akin to meat. Consequently, Seitan is frequently employed in many dishes where meat might otherwise be used.

Steamed: A method of cooking in which food is cooked by water which has been heated to the boiling point and thus converted to steam. This steam is trapped while in contact with the food by means of a lid or cover - an extremely healthy way to prepare cooked food.

Tofu: Soybean curd, or-to be more succinct, cheese made from soy milk. A food quite high in protein and native to Asian cultures. Tofu comes in different textures such as soft or firm and so can be used in many different ways. Soft Tofu is best employed in custards or puddings, whereas firm Tofu is better for stir fry or recipes where you need the tofu to hold together. Tofu is somewhat bland by itself, but is delicious when seasoned. The campaign to discredit tofu by the meat and dairy industries has been quite successful in the West. However, one and a half billion Asians can't be wrong. Anyway, what's the heart attack rate in Asia compared to here?

Tempeh: A fermented soybean product native to Indonesia. The soybeans are inoculated with a culture called rhizopus, which is grown on hibiscus leaves, and which gives it its unique flavor. Tempeh can be prepared in a number of ways, and is often mixed with grains and vegetables.

Vegan: One who excludes all animal products, such as meat, fish, fowl, eggs, and dairy products, from the diet. Many vegans also eschew the use of animal products in other areas of their life as well, such as clothing made from leather or wool.

Index

E

F

G

H

I

J

INDEX BY LOCATION

Planet One
San Loco
Sanctuary
Souen
Two Boots
Village East
Whole Earth Bakery And
Kitchen
Zen Palate

Financial District
Café American
Govinda's
Healthful Essence
Mizrachi
Salad Bowl
Scallion's

Gramercy Park
Bachué
Doctor Squeeze
Health Pub
Madras Mahal
Mavalli Palace
Wok Naturally

Harlem
Dining At Rubi's
Lenox Avenue Health Food
Restaurant
Strictly Roots
Uptown Juice Bar

Midtown East
Eri's Café
Good Food Café
Great American
Health Bar
Salad Bowl
Salad Daze
Teva Natural Foods

Vege Vege II

Midtown West
Great American
Health Bar
Naturworks
Salad Bowl
Vega House
Vegetable Garden
Vegetarian Heaven
Zen Palate

Queens
Annam Brahma
Bamboo Garden
Knish Nosh
Quantum Leap
Salad Bowl
Smile Of The Beyond
Udupi Palace

Staten Island
Dairy Palace

Upper East Side
Burritoville
Candle Café
Good Health Café
Healthy Candle
Hong Kong Vegetarian
Plum Tree

Upper West Side
Bennie's
(formerly Café Bloom)
Bertha's
Blue Nile
Café Viva
Eden Rock
Freddie & Pepper's
Indian Delhi

Josie's
Josephina
Mana
Natural Food Bar
Nutrisserie Deli
Ozu
Tamarind Seed

West Village
Apple
Benny's Burritos
Boostan
Burritoville
Caravan Of Dreams
DojoII
Eva's
Integral Yoga
Quantum Leap
Taqueria
Temple In The Village
Village Natural
VP 2
VP 2–Go
Whole Wheat And Wild
Berries

INDEX BY RACE, CREED OR NATIONAL ORIGIN

African
Abyssinia
Blue Nile
Planet One

African–American
Dining At Rubi's
Nyota's Ting
Uptown Juice Bar

Asian
Bamboo Garden
Hong Kong Vegetarian
House Of Vegetarian
Hunan Delight
New Garden
Red Hot Szechuan
Vega House
Vege Vege II
Vegetarian Heaven
VP–II
VP–2–Go
VP–III
Wok Naturally
Zen Palate

Best Places To Hallucinate
San Loco

Cajun
Two Boots

Corsican
Le Poeme

Ersatz American
Apple

Indian
Annam Brahma
Indian Delhi
Madras Mahal
Mavalli Palace
Udupi Palace

Italian
Café Viva
Freddie & Pepper's
Two Boots

Knisheries
Knish Nosh
Mrs. Stahl's
Yonah Shimmel's

Kosher
American Café
Bamboo Garden
Brighton Beach Dairy
Café Kapulsky
Corner Café
Dairy Palace
Famous Pita
Gourmet Café
Knish Nosh
Madras Mahal
Main Event
Mathilda's Muffins
Mizrachi
Ratner's
Shem Tov

Taam Eden
Teva Natural Foods
Vege Vege II
Vegetarian Heaven
Weiss' Kosher Dairy

Live Music
Bell Café
Caravan of Dreams

Macrobiotic
Angelica Kitchen
Eri's Café
Healthy Henrietta's
Mana
Ozu
Plum Tree
Souen

Mexican
Benny's Burritos
Burritoville
Harry's Burritos
Healthy Henrietta's
San Loco
Taqueria

Middle Eastern
Boostan
Bennie's
Eden Rock
Eva's
Moustache
Mr. Falafel
Naturworks
Oasis

Non-Smoking
Angelica Kitchen

Caravan of Dreams
Eri's Café
Eva's
Good Food Café
Harry's Burritos
Healthy Henrietta's
House Of Vegetarian
Luma
Madras Mahal
Nosmo King
Ozu
Planet One
Plum Tree
Quantum Leap
Scallion's
Souen
Temple In The Village
Village East
Village Natural
VP–2–Go
Whole Wheat And Wild
Berries
Zen Palate

Open Real Late
Bell Café
Dojo (I & II)
San Loco

Places To Find "the Lord"
Temple In The Village
Govinda's

Places To Find Enlighten-ment
Annam Brahma
Sanctuary

Places My Cousin Melvin Likes
Boostan

Places Where You Can Eat With Your Hands
Abyssinia
Blue Nile

Places The Yuppies Like
Luma
Nosmo King
Zen Palate
Zucchini

Restaurants That Share A Name With A T.V. Show
Quantum Leap

Vegan
Angelica Kitchen
Bachué
Caravan of Dreams
Everything Natural
Everything Vital
Health Pub
I Rankin' Ital
Plum Tree
Save The Children
Scallion's
Souen
Strictly Roots
VP–2
VP–2–Go
VP-III
Vege Vege II

West Indian
Healthful Essence
Everything Natural
Everything Vital
I Rankin' Ital
Kings Vegetarian
Lenox Avenue Health Food
Restaurant
Liveth's Delight
Save The Children
Steve & Sons
Strictly Roots
Vegetarian Delights
West Indian Vegetarian & Seafood Restaurant

ONE MORE THING

Notice is hereby given: Things change.

We live in an evolving, expanding universe, of which New York City is the hub.

However, if you send a self–addressed, stamped envelope to us at:

Vegetarian Dining in NYC
P.O. Box 845
Brooklyn, NY 11230

You'll receive a free update on recent closings and openings. See you next edition. Bonne chance.

Dramatis Personae

Arthur S. Brown is an actor, singer, comic, former NYC taxi-driver, publisher, man of letters (a,b,c...), bon-vivant, native New Yorker, father, all 'round swell guy, evangelical vegetarian, and exceedingly modest person. In the words of Buckminster Fuller, "I think I am a verb."

Barbara Holmes earned her B.S. in nutrition from Brooklyn College and works for a Brooklyn W.I.C. program. She follows a plant-centered diet. She's also a mother.

They're married and have one wonderful child.

BOOKS WITH DISCOUNTS

Vegetarian Dining in NYC retails for $8.95. To pay less, team up with your friends.

20% disount if you order at least   4 books: pay just $7.16

40% discount if you order at least   10 books: pay just $5.37

60% discount if you order at least   60 books: pay just $3.58

Because of these discounts, do *not* order 3 books (order 4 instead); do not order 40-59 books (order 60 instead).

How many books would you like? _____ Write their total cost here $ _____

Address

Print the name and address where you want the books sent

If you're a resident of N.Y.C, please enclose 8.25% sales tax. "Render onto Caeser what is Caeser's ..."

Shipping

We ship anywhere! Regular U.S. Snail will cost u nuttin' ! It's on da house! Our standard practice is to ship 4th Class Book Rate. Takes about 1-2 weeks to most of the U.S.A and about 6 weeks elsewhere. Other forms of shipping (like U.P.S. or Airmail) will cost you a little bit of scratch (not too much). For U.P.S., please add on $1.00 extra per book. Takes about 2 days-1 week.

T-Shirts

If you would like a beautiful full color, cotton T-shirt displaying the front and back cover of this lovely book, send $15 and indicate your size (S, M, L). Allow 2-3 weeks for delivery. Free book with every T-shirt! Wot a deal!!

3rd Edition - Cheap!

Why not order as many copies as you like of the "Classic" 3rd Edition. Only $3.50 per copy (originally $8.95)! Wow!

Last, but not Least

Send check or M.O. made out to *Callaloo Press, P.O. Box 845, Brooklyn, NY 11230.*

BOOKS WITH DISCOUNTS

Vegetarian Dining in NYC retails for $8.95. To pay less, team up with your friends.

20% disount if you order at least   4 books: pay just $7.16

40% discount if you order at least   10 books: pay just $5.37

60% discount if you order at least   60 books: pay just $3.58

Because of these discounts, do *not* order 3 books (order 4 instead); do not order 40-59 books (order 60 instead).

How many books would you like? _____ Write their total cost here $ _____

Address
Print the name and address where you want the books sent

If you're a resident of N.Y.C, please enclose 8.25% sales tax. "Render onto Caeser what is Caeser's ..."

Shipping
We ship anywhere! Regular U.S. Snail will cost u nuttin' ! It's on da house! Our standard practice is to ship 4th Class Book Rate. Takes about 1-2 weeks to most of the U.S.A and about 6 weeks elsewhere. Other forms of shipping (like U.P.S. or Airmail) will cost you a little bit of scratch (not too much). For U.P.S., please add on $1.00 extra per book. Takes about 2 days-1 week.

T-Shirts
If you would like a beautiful full color, cotton T-shirt displaying the front and back cover of this lovely book, send $15 and indicate your size (S, M, L). Allow 2-3 weeks for delivery. Free book with every T-shirt! Wot a deal!

3rd Edition - Cheap!
Why not order as many copies as you like of the "Classic" 3rd Edition. Only $3.50 per copy (originally $8.95)! Wow!

Last, but not Least
Send check or M.O. made out to *Callaloo Press, P.O. Box 845, Brooklyn, NY 11230.*

BOOKS WITH DISCOUNTS

Vegetarian Dining in NYC retails for $8.95. To pay less, team up with your friends.

20% disount if you order at least   4 books: pay just $7.16

40% discount if you order at least   10 books: pay just $5.37

60% discount if you order at least   60 books: pay just $3.58

Because of these discounts, do *not* order 3 books (order 4 instead); do not order 40-59 books (order 60 instead).

How many books would you like? _____ Write their total cost here $ _____

Address
Print the name and address where you want the books sent

If you're a resident of N.Y.C, please enclose 8.25% sales tax. "Render onto Caeser what is Caeser's ..."

Shipping
We ship anywhere! Regular U.S. Snail will cost u nuttin' ! It's on da house! Our standard practice is to ship 4th Class Book Rate. Takes about 1-2 weeks to most of the U.S.A and about 6 weeks elsewhere. Other forms of shipping (like U.P.S. or Airmail) will cost you a little bit of scratch (not too much). For U.P.S., please add on $1.00 extra per book. Takes about 2 days-1 week.

T-Shirts
If you would like a beautiful full color, cotton T-shirt displaying the front and back cover of this lovely book, send $15 and indicate your size (S, M, L). Allow 2-3 weeks for delivery. Free book with every T-shirt! Wot a deal!!

3rd Edition - Cheap!
Why not order as many copies as you like of the "Classic" 3rd Edition. Only $3.50 per copy (originally $8.95)! Wow!

Last, but not Least
Send check or M.O. made out to *Callaloo Press, P.O. Box 845, Brooklyn, NY 11230.*

NOTES

NOTES

NOTES